23 DAYS OF INTENSIVE CARE: *a story of miracles*

Overcoming Medical Disorders and Tragedies

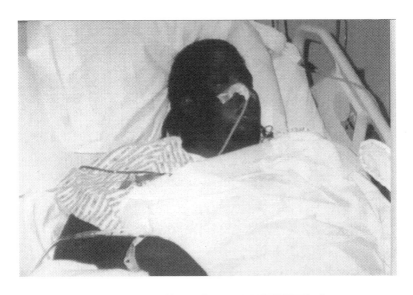

ZON G. QUEWEA

iUniverse, Inc.
New York   Bloomington

**23 Days of Intensive Care: a story of miracles
Overcoming Medical Disorders and Tragedies**

The information, ideas, and suggestions in this book are not intended
as a substitute for professional medical advice. Before following any
suggestions contained in this book, you should consult your personal
physician. Neither the author nor the publisher shall be liable or
responsible for any loss or damage allegedly arising as a consequence of
your use or application of any information or suggestions in this book.

iUniverse books may be ordered through booksellers or by contacting:

iUniverse
1663 Liberty Drive
Bloomington, IN 47403
www.iuniverse.com
1-800-Authors (1-800-288-4677)

Because of the dynamic nature of the Internet, any Web addresses or links
contained in this book may have changed since publication and may no longer be
valid. The views expressed in this work are solely those of the author and do not
necessarily reflect the views of the publisher, and the publisher hereby disclaims
any responsibility for them.

ISBN: 978-1-4502-2327-0 (sc)
ISBN: 978-1-4502-2325-6 (dj)
ISBN: 978-1-4502-2326-3 (ebook)

Printed in the United States of America

iUniverse rev. date: 05/18/2010

CONTENTS

PART II
A REFLECTION ON THE PAST; FURTHER FINDINGS

ACKNOWLEDGMENT

SOME DOCTORS SAID MY WIFE'S RECOVERY was beyond their capabilities; others said she was a walking miracle. I wrote this book as witness to a miracle of God which, like the miracles recorded in the past, continue in the present and will no doubt still occur in the future. Our God is a never changing God. Therefore my sincere gratitude goes to… the Lord for His miracle, His timely intervention in restoring my wife's life, a development that was initially unthinkable to the mind of most people. During the darkest period of our family life, the Lord came in and brought light to our dull and lifeless home. My son John would have been motherless today, but Our Heavenly Father said, "No."

My family is grateful to be part of Your body, the Church. The greatest decision we have ever made was to know you, Our Lord.

To the nurses at Labor and Delivery—you took care of baby John with the same care his mother would have given him after birth. I will never forget you. The Rapid Responders, you were rapid indeed on that day. You did what you could. To the nurses on ICU 2600 Level, and ICU 2700 Level, the intensive care you provided with God's guidance was effective. I will also not forget the nurses on the Third Level. It was there that I first came across a nurse who had asked me to pray with her for my wife's recovery. And to the doctors who provided care directly or indirectly, I recognize your effort. To me, you all have been God's instrument in saving my wife's life. I honor your work and I am thankful to the Lord for His miracle to make your work shine.

To the Central Church of Christ, Oakland Avenue, Johnson City, Tennessee—you not only prayed ceaselessly, you also did what a biological family would do. You cried with me, you laughed with me and you were there every step of the way to the end. Your involvement was a reminder of the teachings of the apostles' doctrines as spelled out in the Book of Acts—you met my needs in all aspects—physical and spiritual. Keep holding unto the unchanging hands of the Lord. May the Lord multiply His body daily.

To the Centre International d'Evangelisation/Tabernacle Bethel Israel Church of Burkina Faso, Ouagadougou, West Africa—there are thousands of you I do not know even to this day, though you may have known my wife. The time you spent in your prayer tower, praying and fasting for my wife, was not in vain. It was your desire to see her recovered and she did indeed recover. You not only prayed for my wife and my baby, you also prayed for me. My words of appreciation may not be enough, but like Paul said to the church in Phillippi, *"My Lord shall supply your need according to His glory in Christ Jesus."*

To my father-in-law, Dr. Mamadou Philippe Karambiri, Senior Pastor and founder of Centre International d'Evangelisation/Tabernacle Bethel Israel Church, Ouagadougou, Burkina Faso, West Africa—of the 23 days of intensive care, you spent 18 of those days with me physically. But prior to this time, you were thousands of miles from me, far away in Africa, yet you strengthened me through your words of encouragement and prayers. You rearranged your busy schedule to attend to my wife's illness. When you arrived, together we worried, together we prayed and together we gained strength and today, there is laughter. As a man of God, the Lord will never abandon you. Your ceaseless prayers and devotion for the recovery of your daughter, Daniella, my wife, were answered.

To Dr. Paul Kamolnick, Associate Professor of Sociology, my former Professor at East Tennessee State University—for calling to check on me, to find out my wife's condition. Your socially sensitive approach to human plight helped to keep me strong.

To Bernard Zougouri, Pastor, Centre International d'Evangelisation/ Tabernacle Bethel Israel Church, USA, Atlanta, Georgia's branch—your unwavering commitment in prayers to see my wife recovered is unforgettable. You stepped beyond the lines of an in-law. You are more than a friend and a brother. For several sleepless nights you and your wife drove over 400 miles to come and see us and pray for recovery during my wife's worsening condition. Your encouragement was even more important. When my wife could not talk, open her eyes or even breathe on her own and entirely depended on a ventilator, you did not see a dead person. You saw a mother who was asleep preparing for the next day to care for her newborn baby. You took a pen and a sheet of paper and wrote a note in French, you placed it on her pillow and said, "Tomorrow when she gets up she will read it and call me." Yes, I am sure you have had several of those calls.

To Pastor Afra Lengar—you heard the news at your home in Atlanta, Georgia and took it on head-on. Like Pastor Zougouri, you also drove from Atlanta, Georgia to spend a whole night with me at the hospital. Even though you had just left work that day, you tarried with me all night long. Your God certainly saw you and many others, and answered your prayers.

To Pastor John Korsinah of Ghana, Accra, West Africa, who came into our life through David, my wife's younger brother, at the time when we were in desperate need of a child—his desire to see us have a child was infused with constant prayer and fasting almost every day. When you heard that my wife had collapsed from blood clots to her lungs after a day of labor, you spent days in the mountains of Ghana again praying and fasting. You called me every week to assure me that you were with me in prayers.

To Mrs. Pauline Chevalier—you flew all the way from Africa, to quickly fill in and become a surrogate mother to baby John. Baby John was entrusted into your hands from the hospital. When the time for his discharge came, there was no one at home to care for him. I pleaded with the hospital staff to allow me some time. When you came, you touched my heart. You also kept showing me scriptures and telling me of your dreams that God would not let me down. I could not ask for more.

To Kabou Nignan—your school became less important to you when you came down and helped in every way possible. Baby John's first set of hospital visits were yours. For weeks, you took care of Baby John, and prayed with us. Also, Nina Kabore and Michelle Gayechuway—you all traveled from Texas to help me as well as pray, as did others. Your presence gave me the necessary courage to stay strong.

To the Liberian Community of Johnson City, Tennessee—your arrival at the hospital on a daily basis caused the nurses to realize that my wife and I belong to a group. You filled the waiting room and even my wife's hospital room. There were times when nurses complained about congestion; there were other times they had to get us a bigger room to accommodate you. It was your desire to see my wife, your friend, recovered. Your wishes came through. I felt your concerns; I appreciate you. To Younger Duanah specifically—you were not frustrated when told to leave by the nurses. You kept coming again and again. You left your job many times to sit with my wife, to bathe her and to clothe her. And John and Oretha Kollie—you were with me throughout those days. Even in my absence from the hospital you were there praying for my wife. You all gave me unconditional friendship.

Not forgetting Henderson W. Bennah, Deacon, Thankful Baptist Church of Johnson City—for his prayers for my wife's recovery, and to Mr. and Mrs. Seydou Dao who traveled from Africa to visit us at the hospital, prayed with us and encouraged us.

There are some of you who went out of your way to do all you could. Forgive me if I forgot you in this book. The Lord saw all your work and your effort is recognized.

To my editor at Kora Press, Joanna Francis, for her prompt work and sensitivity in helping me preserve my unique voice. To Martha Rose Woodward for consultation and encouragement as one who has made the journey into the publishing world ahead of me and has helped me to find my own path.

And finally—it is with much love that I dedicate this book to my mother-in-law, Mama Karambiri (now deceased). Many have known her to be Mama due to the love she gave to everyone who met her. During the five years my wife and I prayed and fasted for a child, Mama Karambiri was with us. She even prophesied that the year 2007 was our year of breakthrough when we never thought of having a child. She struggled through her share of tension from her friends and from the pressure my wife faced for being "barren," as they used to say. She was with us throughout our darkest moment and prayed without ceasing until her daughter recovered. A few months after Daniella's health crisis, the Lord called Mama home at the tender age of 59. We believe He loved her and we pray for her soul to rest in perfect peace with Him. Thank you, our blessed Mama, for all you have done. You are truly a mother who cared.

It is my desire that this book reawaken you, the readers, to the miracles of God. We cannot be in denial of the truth as it is written in the Bible. When the Hudson River plane crash happened on January 15th, 2009 and all passengers on board were saved, many of us attributed that to the expertise of the pilot. What we failed to recognize was that the pilot has no ability to keep a plane from sinking even after a difficult landing, until all passengers are rescued, which is what happened. When another plane crashed into the Pacific Ocean, of the 153 passengers on board, a 14-year-old girl was the only survivor. What lesson did we learn from those instances? These instances and many others should have us thinking in a way to rewire our thoughts and recognize the work of the Lord. This book is all about the miracle of God.

PREFACE

On December 8th, 2007, my wife, Daniella Quewea, collapsed suddenly in her hospital bathroom from blood clots to her lungs one day after undergoing a Caesarean section delivery. When the nurses at Labor and Delivery, the Rapid Responders and doctors arrived, they found no pulse and no breathing after a few minutes of resuscitation. She was coded twice and pronounced clinically dead according to the initial report. Other rumors had it that she was dead.

They put her on a stretcher and took her to ICU 2600 Level for further resuscitation. One nurse took me in one of the rooms in the waiting area of the ICU in preparation for the worst news about her death. They prevented me from entering her room. I insisted and they promised me that if it became necessary they would call me to her side. Her situation was so hopeless that my expectation, as I sat in the waiting area, only reflected on the worst possible scenario.

While sitting in the waiting room, Brother Timothy Hall, my preacher from Central Church of Christ of Johnson City, Tennessee, came in shocked and confused. He led me through prayer and committed the situation into God's hands. A few minutes later a doctor came in to let me know that they were doing their best to revive my wife. I requested to be with her in the intensive care unit. He refused initially, but I insisted. He said yes on the condition that if it became necessary they would ask me to leave her room. I agreed and followed him to the room. As I entered the room, my expectation was to see my wife with open eyes, breathing… but unfortunately, I didn't see any of that; she barely clung to life, heavily ventilated, between life and death. It was then that I realized that only a miracle from God could revive her. No doctor or nurse would comment on anything as I kept looking around to find someone who would be willing to tell me something about her condition from a medical standpoint.

I sat spellbound in my wife's presence in almost perfect silence. The farthest my mind could go wandering was to the new journey the day had brought to me. It was a journey of total panic, tears, distress and confusion. It was a journey where faith and prayer were robustly tested while only a miracle of God could possibly bring relief.

Note from the Chief Executive Officer of the Johnson City Medical Center (John W. Melton):

"I was notified by the Central Church of Christ that Daniella Quewea was in the hospital at Johnson City Medical Center where she was delivering her first baby. Being the Chief Executive Officer (CEO) of the hospital and member of the Central Church, I was often notified by the Church about any member of the Church that was in the hospital so that I might go by and visit if I had the time. I was told that Daniella was in labor so I went to the labor room to see if I could be of any help to her. I stopped by our gift shop and bought Daniella a dozen red roses and took them with me to the labor room. She had relatives visiting so I left the flowers in her room with them. Her nurse and relatives told me that Daniella had problems after the delivery and that she was in our Critical Care Unit. One of the nurses told me that it would take a miracle for her to ever leave the hospital alive.

"I witnessed Zon on his knees beside the bed of Daniella for days—praying without ceasing. Zon and Daniella taught me the power of prayer and that there are miracles that happen today—I witnessed this miracle happen right before my eyes."

The next 23 days on, her condition would still remain tenuous and doctors would suggest to a brother from the church, who was also a member of the senior management staff at the hospital, that her chances of survival were close to zero. Later, when the Lord restored my wife's life, that friend asked my wife, "Did you know you were dead?" He went on to say, "You are a walking miracle."

Looking back, my wife survived the onslaught of what started even before her pregnancy as high blood pressure, then led to a high-risk pregnancy, preeclampsia and finally blood clots to the lungs only through God's miracle. I believe the successful journey through each of these disorders took a miracle of God. Gradually coming out of the situation by His grace, another shock whacked us. It was a tragedy.

My wife's Mom, Mama Karambiri died of unknown causes at the age of 59. We were already frail; having survived previous events associated with my wife's illness and were on the verge of a breaking point. It was a delicate issue to inform my wife about her mother's death. Together with some family members we broke the news to her, but God, being a wonder-working God, prevented the situation from erupting. As the psalmist put it, *"The Lord is close to the brokenhearted and saves those who are crushed in spirit"* (Psalm 34:18).

PART I
ILLNESS, INTENSIVE CARE AND RECOVERY

CHAPTER 1
THE SURGE OF DISORDERS;
HIGH BLOOD PRESSURE

"Though the mountains be shaken and the hills be removed, yet my unfailing love for you will not be shaken, nor my covenant of peace be removed, says the Lord, who has compassion on you."

Isaiah 54:10

"When you pass through the waters, I will be with you; and when you pass through the rivers, they will not sweep over you. When you walk through the fire, you will not be burned; the flames will not set you ablaze. For I am the Lord, your God, the Holy one of Israel, your Savior."

Isaiah 43:2-3

MY NAME IS ZON QUEWEA; I was born in Liberia, West Africa to the union of MeDolly and David Jones Quewea. I attended primary, middle, and high schools in Liberia. I became a Christian in 1987 and have since been a member of the Church of Christ. I fled to Ghana, Accra, West Africa in 1990 due to the deadly Civil War in Liberia that killed over 150,000 people. In 1998, after my stay in Ghana, I had the opportunity to come to the United States of America to further my education and for a better life. I studied at East Tennessee State University and earned a B.S. in Sociology, Political Science and an M.A. in Liberal Studies.

In my heart, I longed for a companion, a wife, someone to love and someone to love me and I dreamed of a true family full of children with relatives and friends always around us sharing in our happiness. One day, in 2001, after a long conversation on the subject of marriage with my cousin Johnny Gayechuway, now in the US Army, I learned the name Daniella Karambiri. News of this woman and her characteristics intrigued me. I found myself often thinking of her and wondering if she might be the one chosen for me by God to be my wife.

In order to meet Daniella Karambiri, I traveled thousands of miles to Africa, Burkina Faso, Ouagadougou where she lived. When I first met her, I felt a bit shy because she stands an inch taller than my height of 5' 6". But, we found that our love was blind as our engagement came quickly when the chemistry between us showed great signs of compatibility. Daniella immediately developed two nicknames she preferred to call me by: "Sweetie" and "Daddy." I began to call her "Sweetie" as well. But after the wedding, I changed the nickname to "D.Q." for Daniella Quewea. My wife has three siblings: Sarah, the eldest, followed by Samuel and David, the youngest son. Her parents are Dr. Pastor, Mamadou P. Karambiri and her mother's name was Marie-Sophie Karambiri.

In 2005 I became a naturalized US Citizen. I live a joyful life in Knoxville, Tennessee with my family, which, at the time of this writing, has grown to include Daniella, Baby John, born December 7, 2007 and Emmanuel, our second child born January 10, 2010.

Here is my family's story:

Daniella and I got married in June 2002. As part of our plans, like most couples, we wanted to have children. My wife became pregnant in the first month of our marriage. Two months into the pregnancy she had a miscarriage. Relying on an ultrasound result that showed that nothing was found in her womb after the miscarriage, we chose not to go forward with a Dilation and Curettage (D&C), even though the doctors advised us to do so. A D&C is a procedure done surgically after a first trimester miscarriage. One of the reasons for refusal hinged on the risks and complications involved, such as heavy bleeding or hemorrhaging, weakening of the cervix, laceration and an infection in the uterus or other pelvic organs. Until 2007, Daniella and I tried fruitlessly to initiate another pregnancy. During those five years of trials and failures, some of our friends and family members subjected my wife to excessive mockery on grounds of barrenness.

As you will read later in this book in Part II, Chapter One in detail, the issue of barrenness was one of the factors that contributed to the trouble we had later when pregnancy finally came. To be an African and ignore the problems of barrenness you must have a strong heart. This is so because in African marriages, children are the main emphasis. If a woman cannot have children, she is often derided, divorced or has to put up with her husband taking a second wife. Being barren causes untold suffering to an African woman. Often adoption is out of the question.

With so much emotional baggage to bear—the tension associated with the attempts to have children and the pressure exerted on my wife—she started declining in health. From the stress of it all, her blood pressure went up to a high of 190/101. At the same time she began developing abnormal weight gains.

At one point, she weighed as much as 330 pounds and stood at 5 feet 7 inches in height. Even with the weight gains, my wife was not subjected to regular treatment for the high blood pressure; neither did she seriously consider losing weight. As it became obvious that the situation was worsening, we decided on a regular treatment pattern for both problems.

To our amazement, it was in the middle of this treatment that she became pregnant again. The unexpected pregnancy caused us to regain hope for our dream of having children to come true, but at the same time, it also raised more questions about what to expect. Our concerns were that the high blood pressure had not gone away completely, as the numbers continued to fluctuate. With no medical background, we began wondering, even before meeting her doctor, as to the effect of high blood pressure on a pregnant woman and what it could do to the baby's health. When we visited a CVS store or Wal-Mart to check her blood pressure, the numbers were always dangerously high. The good news was the numbers were down a little from the first reading, as reported above. We continued to see variations in the numbers—sometimes the reading would be 160/90 or 165/85. But whenever she visited her doctor for checkups, the numbers bounced even more.

The effect of high blood pressure on a pregnancy can be dire, as we found out later. My wife's doctor was kind enough to explain to us the influence of blood pressure on a pregnancy. It was the kind of news we really didn't want to hear but were obliged to listen to. According to her doctor, a pregnancy with high blood pressure may cause less blood to flow to the placenta, which would indicate that the fetus is receiving less nutrients and not enough oxygen for its needs. When this happens, she noted, it has the potential to slow down the growth of the fetus. The second problem my wife was facing was that she is 5 feet 7 inches in height and at the time weighed 330 pounds. The normal weight for a female of her height is, at most, 168 pounds. Daniella was almost double her normal weight level. That was another reason for serious concerns.

Week after week she had different readings during checkups. As the pregnancy evolved, her doctor's visits became even more frequent, sometimes twice a week. As a college student, her regular doctor's appointments began interrupting her classes at a crucial time during the semester. I assumed that if blood pressure could be treated by surgery, my wife would have opted for that to avoid the many trips to the hospital so that she would be able to pay attention to her lessons. But even more important was no longer the concern about her classes. What became central to us was the health of the unborn baby, the developing fetus. She was prepared to suspend classes for a semester or even a year. Knowing that with blood pressure treatment there are no quick fixes, we had to take it one day at a time for the sake of the baby we had longed for.

Given what we had already learned about high blood pressure, we were convinced that it was deadly serious. Most doctors view it as a silent killer, and dealing with it requires an extra level of care and effort. We were told stories of people with a history of high blood pressure and they were devastating. Those who treated it lightly often ended up with other forms of health problems, such as heart attacks, heart diseases, strokes, and they sometimes developed kidney problems. High blood pressure puts pregnant women at a higher risk of low birth weight and early delivery. So, managing such a problem during pregnancy is like constructing a bridge over troubled waters.

News of Daniella's health became grimmer by the day. It was truly a moment of reckoning. Honestly, we had no idea we would be headed in this direction—having to wonder and worry about high blood pressure as part of our dinnertime conversation. My wife continued to have severe headaches and rapid weight gains as time passed, even though she was being treated for high blood pressure. We thought these were conventional high blood pressure symptoms, but that only testifies to our scant knowledge of healthcare practices. When she went to see her doctor to check her blood pressure, the initial reading was so high they could not let her go home. They asked her to stay for a while and took another reading later. She called me to let me know what was going on. She said it would be okay and that I shouldn't bother coming to the doctor's office. Finally, a second test was done and the result was not encouraging.

ELEVATED BLOOD PRESSURE

MY WIFE WAS TOLD THAT HER BLOOD pressure had elevated from mild to a severe level. The doctors decided to put her on high-risk pregnancy status. The phrase "high-risk" doesn't need further explanation, even for those outside the medical profession, like me. Obviously, we were into a more intense struggle against the disorder. We knew that if nothing was done to resolve the problem, not only the baby's life would have been in danger but the mother's as well. Most doctors, if not all, apply the phrase "high-risk pregnancy" to confirm the need for constant treatment. They intend to make sure that a pregnant woman gets special attention during her high-risk pregnancy. In that situation, they keep a close watch over her, monitoring the condition as frequently as possible to detect further complications.

However, while special monitoring of the pregnancy was necessary with this condition, what high-risk pregnancy really means, according to the doctor, includes a whole host of problems: infection, hepatitis C, HIV and other sexually transmitted diseases such as syphilis. Other issues at play include sickle-cell anemia, lupus and asthma. Also a woman with a past history of miscarriages, diabetes and high blood pressure could be at a higher risk during her pregnancy—the list is endless. Being told that my wife was at a high-risk level made us cringe in spirit, but as far as we can remember, of the list of many different possible diseases that lead to high-risk, my wife had experienced only a few: a miscarriage and high blood pressure. But even with these two problems, it was enough to accept the fact that we had to work harder to deal with these issues.

Looking back, our days appeared to be punctuated by bouts of varying and dangerous diagnoses; it was a period of meditating to consider the next step forward to confront each week and month ahead with every level of seriousness. As we worked through our remaining options to treat the elevated blood pressure, every effort appeared to be in vain. There was little or no improvement to the level of blood pressure.

PREECLAMPSIA

WHEN WE FINALLY WENT BACK TO SEE my wife's doctor for her regular check up, he told us an astonishing story that further devastated us and instantly became the most awful moment. When the results came back, the doctor took us into one of the rooms and said that my wife was diagnosed with preeclampsia. After he had said that, he told us he would be back in a minute to tell us what to do next. I had not heard the word preeclampsia until that moment. Like me, my wife was also a novice regarding preeclampsia.

What it was, its effects, severity, the prevention and treatment didn't sound that serious to us as we stood there before the doctor, puzzled. In my mind, as I struggled to figure out what it was, my only assumption was that if this were a serious health problem like HIV, AIDS, cancer etc., many people, including myself, outside of the health professions, would have had some knowledge of it. To me, such assumption made logical sense due to the fact that anything that causes a public health problem is publicized and people are advised how to prevent or, if possible, cure it.

We waited for the doctor for a little over 30 minutes as he consulted his colleagues and other members of the high-risk team. While waiting and talking, the only concern we had was the health of the unborn baby. So I suggested to my wife to ask for an ultrasound when the doctor came back. We wanted to be sure of the baby's health status because of the high blood pressure. In the middle of our discussion the doctor arrived and laid out the details of what preeclampsia is, its effects on pregnancy, its commonality with high blood pressure, who is more likely to have it and at what age it is prevalent and a host of other symptoms that would follow.

At that moment, the information was so shocking that the details refused to sink into my head or my wife's head. In his concluding statement, the doctor said something that made the details much more real. Having described preeclampsia, he said, "The only cure to preeclampsia is delivery, possibly by C-section." He went on to say, "With this condition we have to put her on bed rest." The bed rest option was a good idea but it was also a decision to choose between two equally important issues.

The time of the diagnosis was the month of November. My wife's academic year as a student was soon coming to an end. The question became, what do we do? It was a tough decision; we sought further options that could allow her to complete the month of November in school when lectures and some of her final examinations would be over. We left the hospital that day with the understanding that her doctor's visits would have to be even more frequent to keep a close watch on her.

Looking back, the compromise we made was probably a misstep, as things soon turned out. About two weeks later my wife received a call from her doctor while in class, telling her that an appointment had been made and she needed to come in. Again, I went with her. The first thing they wanted to do was an ultrasound. They wanted to check how the baby was doing. The first nurse that administered the ultrasound told us that she needed to call a doctor to see what was going on with the baby. The doctor arrived and from his reading of what he saw on the screen, he made the decision to immediately admit my wife to hospital that night which was December 6th. He said that the baby's growth was declining and if possible, a C-section was going to be done that same day.

It became unavoidable at that time; school was no longer a priority. We went home, packed some items, said a few words of prayer in our living room and headed back to the hospital. My wife's initial due date was between December 20th and 22nd. Her dad had planned to be there to see his first grandchild being born. More than likely, not all of the preparations we had made would be completed, like, for example, the naming ceremony—a ritual observed in many cultures around the world, where members of the couple's families, friends and others would gather to introduce the newborn baby to the community. We had planned to do it in a Christian way, to have my father-in-law lead the ceremony with the reading of some scriptures, singing of hymns, followed by prayers and then officially naming the baby. In some African traditions, a naming ceremony is performed to bring the child under the protection of those present at the ceremony. But here, in our Christian way, it was God's protection we would be invoking.

Because John was his first grandchild, we had extended the opportunity of naming him to my wife's dad. But the new schedule of the baby's birth meant that there was no way he could be there on time since he had planned other events with his church prior to the due date. The only thing he could do was to give us the baby's name. I phoned him to ask about the baby's name. He told me to read from the gospel of Luke 1:13-17. From these passages, we derive the name of our child—it is John.

But worse than the disappointment that Pastor Karambiri could not arrive on time for the birth was the fact that the doctors had suspected danger for our child. Nothing could console us, especially with the news that the baby's survival was a fifty-fifty chance coupled with the unexpected new schedule they gave us for delivery. There were no other choices but to conform to their decision.

CHAPTER 2
DELIVERY BY CESAREAN SECTION

IT ALL CAME DOWN TO THE MONTH of December. Precisely on December 6th my wife was admitted at the hospital. The most likely delivery option we had was a C-section due to the high-risk nature of her pregnancy. The doctors had to consider the options between the initial choice and normal delivery on the condition that if her blood pressure was low enough, a C-section could be avoided. Being admitted, they had the chance to monitor the baby's health and also the mother's blood pressure level. The process began during the late morning hours to about 1:00 A.M., December 7th. During this time, with my limited medical knowledge, I asked all the necessary questions regarding the risk involved during and after the operation. According to the doctor, the worse case scenario leads to blood clots with death being a possible outcome.

With the prospect of a C-section being unavoidable, my wife called back home to inform her parents in Burkina Faso, West Africa. They were in agreement, perhaps having no other options available. By 1:30 A.M. the doctor with whom I had had the initial discussion, came in and tapped me on the shoulder and in a calm but solemn voice said that the baby's health was declining rapidly and it was necessary to save his life; therefore, they would have to perform the C-section immediately. My wife and I prayed briefly when he left to get a wheelchair to take her into the operating room. My wife requested that her obstetrician/gynecologist (OBGYN) be present for the operation. They told her that she was already on the way to the hospital. She arrived in about five minutes. I requested to go with them to the operating room. They agreed but called me in about ten minutes later. At exactly 2:10 A.M. the operation was successfully completed, and the baby was born. It took roughly an additional 10 to 15 minutes to complete the final stages of dressing.

My wife was taken back to her room but remained unconscious for a few seconds while the assigned nurse tried to revive her. She was okay a few minutes later. The fear of danger during the operation had vanished; we now had a fine son. So it was time to spread the good news across the continents. The first call was made to Africa to inform Daniella's parents and, subsequently, the word spread here in the US to other friends within and out of state. By about 11 A.M. on the morning of December 7th, congratulatory messages, cards, phone calls, gift items and visitors from our local community prevented us from having any privacy in the delivery room. The room was jam-packed with people. I randomly picked some of the congratulatory messages for the book:

"For the proud parents of a new baby boy: it is wonderful to hear the news of the little addition to your family! Parenting is such a rewarding adventure as you come to know all the characteristics God has given your child. Your son is a gift—enjoy every moment."

"Just think: your son is here not by chance, but by God's choosing. His hands formed him and made him the person he is. God compares him to no one else. He is one of a kind. Your son will lack nothing that God's grace can give him. God has allowed your son to be here at this time in history to fulfill his special purpose for this generation."

The last on the list came from the highest official of government of my state, the State of Tennessee. Perhaps it is a tradition in Tennessee that every newborn receives a welcome card from the state's governor, just like when one becomes naturalized to be a US citizen he or she is welcomed by the President of the United States. We were honored to receive the following inspiring message from the Governor and the First Lady:

"Congratulations on the new addition to your family; as parents, we know how excited you must be. Remember, the path to a happy life begins with a healthy baby. Please take your infant to be immunized before two months of age. Again, congratulations on your new arrival." Gov. Phil Bredesen and First Lady Andrea Conte.

These congratulatory messages and others from every level and place quickly flooded our hospital room desk. The festive mood we experienced that morning of December 7th was exciting. It continued throughout the day and extended deep into the night. We had no reason to believe that anything would happen, as the doctor had assured us during our discussion prior to the operation. As a result, the idea of blood clots never crossed our minds. In fact, the nurses had already begun bringing in information on postpartum care that my wife would be taking home with her. They were planning to discharge her on Monday, December 10th, since she appeared to be in a healthy condition.

With my wife's condition, I chose to go to work on that Friday, December 7th at 3 P.M. I returned at 10 P.M. I met many people in the room having fun; some bringing out old stories from the past and making my wife feel so comfortable. There was a jubilant mood and much laughter in the room that kept everyone going. I melted into it and began cracking my own jokes to the point that my wife asked me to go home and leave her alone that night. She also said that because I had been sleeping on the recliner since she was admitted to hospital, it would be better for me to go home and have enough rest that night and return to the hospital the next morning, December 8th. Her request was denied. I told her, I was going to be there with her and the baby. Later, after everyone had left, we had the chance to have some family discussions, and later I went to sleep in my recliner and she also fell asleep from about 1:00 to 2:00 A.M.

Before we slept, we had discussed the possibility of making some arrangements on the following day, which was a Saturday. I was scheduled to be off work on that Saturday and therefore planned to clean up our home in preparation for the baby's arrival in a few days. We slept soundly that night uninterrupted. I did not even turn or toss on my recliner as I had done on previous nights when I would periodically check on my wife. Little did we know that that night would be the last time we would have such a sound sleep for a long time. What we were about to experience in a matter of hours would be life changing.

CHAPTER 3
PREECLAMPSIA;
23 DAYS OF INTENSIVE CARE

DECEMBER 8th
DAY 1
"I CAN'T BREATHE!"

"Give thanks in all circumstances, for this is God's will for Christ Jesus."

1 Thessalonians 5:18

ABOUT 6:30 A.M. I WAS STILL ASLEEP; MY wife got up to go to the bathroom. On her way to the bathroom door, she called me, "Daddy! Daddy! I can't breathe." I answered, "I am calling the nurses now." She said, "No, I will be okay." I didn't listen and quickly alerted the nurses and followed her to the bathroom. Our brief exchanges lasted for about 45 seconds. By the time I got to the bathroom door, within another ten to fifteen seconds, my wife was already helpless, almost falling from the commode. Her speech was slurring, the eyes were rolling over and the body became completely motionless. The nurses were still not coming, so I shouted again and again for help. By then she was sitting on the toilet, foaming from the mouth. I attempted to lower her onto the floor, but I couldn't do that so easily. With my first aid skills, I began administering CPR while the nurses were still on their way. I shouted her name, "D.Q.! D.Q.!" By this time, it was only the vibration of my voice that came back to me in response. It seemed that my wife was already many miles away from me, unwillingly walking out of her life, leaving behind her most cherished dream—Baby John.

The nurses arrived on the scene and saw me bending over my wife administering CPR. They quickly took over and sent for the Rapid Response team. There was no room in the toilet to hold everyone so they decided to move my wife into the open area in front of the nursing station. The Rapid Responders arrived and applied CPR; it failed and they proceeded to apply an automated external defibrillator (AED). That also didn't make any significant progress. As I stood by watching the Rapid Responders doing all they could to resuscitate my wife, it all appeared like a dream to me. I kept shouting "D.Q.! D.Q.! You can't do this to me, D.Q.! D.Q.! You can't do this to Baby John."

Among the group of Rapid Responders was a church brother who attended the same church with me. He heard my voice and seeing me with tears rolling down my cheeks, he shouted in a loud voice, "Brother, be still, I have sent for brother Tim (our preacher) to be with you." With the application of CPR and AED not producing a positive response—no pulse—they decided to rush her to the Intensive Care Unit (2600) Level for further resuscitation. That day, I knew my life had changed forever. Here is a portion of the nurses' account of the occurrence based on my report and what they had witnessed:

"Husband rang call bell at approx. 06:50, husband states pt stated she could not breathe, pt on commode, appears to be having seizure, pt unresponsive, frothy secretion from mouth noted with breathing. Dr. Wilson paged at 06:59 (time on Dr. Wilson's pager was 06:56), Drs Wilson and Doug at pt side in bathroom, Dr. Wilson states they were at pt side when the pager went off, pt placed on floor because she was unable to stand on her own without assistance and needed to be placed in supine position, pt having agonal breathing while on floor, continue to have frothy secretions from mouth, no blood noted at this time in secretions, due to morbid obesity pt very difficult to move or lift, bed sheet placed under pt's shoulders and pelvis to assist with lifting and moving, pt placed back in bed, Rapid Responder team paged at approx. 07:01 and at bedside, pt assessed and noted to be pulseless, code blue called and CPR initiated at 07:06 with code team, Rapid Responders and Dr. Cummings/Obed (anesthesia) present to run code."

December 8th became the beginning of a long journey I was not prepared for; I did not have a clue it was coming. *What had happened to my wife? How was it going to end? What would become of my baby? What should I say to the people in Africa and my wife's parents who were still celebrating the birth of their grandchild? How was I going to explain it if they called to check in on their daughter and grandchild?* These questions and many more brought the reality of the matter to the forefront. When they took my wife to the ICU for further resuscitation, I was forbidden to enter the room where the crew of Rapid Responders and other doctors were doing their best to revive her. They took me into one of the rooms in the waiting area where my preacher met me as soon as he arrived at the hospital. He began to encourage me but I could also feel from his tone of voice that he was in shock because I had informed him the day before of my wife's delivery. He had then promised to put the information on the Church's website where announcements are usually sent to inform the congregation, only to now hear a story of tragedy.

While he was talking with me after a moment of prayer, one of the doctors came in to update me. I told him I wanted to see my wife in the ICU.

Initially he refused, but I insisted. He said, "Okay, but if it becomes necessary, we will ask you to leave." I accepted his condition and went in to sit by her bedside, a routine I was initiating with many more days of discomfort ahead. After a few hours of resuscitation, they found a pulse; a decision was then reached to take the next step. They began testing for the cause that led to her breathing problems and subsequent collapse.

The day had been far spent and my wife was still not responsive, except for the pulse they had detected. Later, during the late afternoon hours, they found that a pulmonary embolism had occurred that led to her condition. This finding answered one of my questions: what had happened to my wife? I would come to know later that pulmonary embolism is a life-threatening medical condition that occurs when a blood clot travels to the lungs and blocks the artery in the process. With this report, I would also remember later that something was left out from the discussion I had with the doctor prior to my wife's operation. What I thought was omitted was the need for post-operative care—the need to prevent possible blood clots. I didn't remember asking that question or I was probably not told what could be done after the C-section to prevent any possible blood clots. I needed answers to this question. Browsing through my wife's medical records, I came across the information that helped answer some of my questions. See intra-operative, and post-operative records in Appendix B.

Walking was recommended after a C-session. The nurses had encouraged her to walk a little each day as she was awaiting her possible discharge on Monday, December 10th, bu that didn't help, as it turned out. A new chapter began; it was only a day earlier when congratulatory messages were coming in. By the nightfall on December 8th (a day later), different kinds of greetings started coming in. Among them are the following:

"Keeping you in our prayers as you recuperate, love. With deep sympathy."

Another one said, "Thinking of you with heart filled with compassion and love…"

It was a day the likes of which I had never experienced in my life. It happened so fast, and it came with no sense of compassion, and indeed it turned an exhilarating moment into sorrow. Until the evening came, I could not gather my mind and I had no words with which to inform my wife's parents who were several thousands of miles away in Africa. A few hours after the incident occurred, Adja, one of our friends in the community, arrived. I asked her to call Africa to inform my wife's people. She could not do it either, but in turn asked me, "What am I going to say to Mama Karambiri or Dad?" She was in tears for the most part of the day while her friend was lying prostrate due to blood clots, having no strength to fight back.

The day ended with no positive signs of survival, with the expectation that my wife would be lucky to see the next day. I guess the doctors gave my wife the benefit of the doubt and had her placed on breathing machines until I would truly believe that my wife was gone and would agree to have the machines switched off. I informed her parents later through Pastor Zougouri, a family friend in Atlanta, Georgia.

As a Christian, the Bible teaches me to give thanks in all circumstances. With my feeble spirit, I reclined by my wife's bed in a new location within the same hospital under different conditions, trying to be thankful to God for the fact that I still had a reason to be thankful. My wife was still with me, even though we could not talk to one another. There were no drops of sleep in my eyes that night. In such a shocking mood, my eyes remained open throughout the night until the next day. That night, as it turned out, was only a rehearsal for many days and weeks ahead. I would be awake for nights and would be speaking to myself as if I were going mad. Sometimes in the middle of this, if a nurse came in, I would manage to catch myself pretending to be quiet. Once he/she stepped out, I would resume my soliloquy. Some of those talks were praises to God; others were my recounting of my misery.

The question of what the next day would bring was only a matter of speculation. But more than anything else, the negative thoughts were making headway in my mind. I am sure everyone who saw my wife on that day, including the doctors, succumbed to the same feelings that I was having.

DECEMBER 9th
DAY 2
BLOOD CLOTS DISCOVERED
POST-OPERATIVE TREATMENT

"New journeys await you. Decisions lie ahead, wondering… what you will do; where you will go, how you will choose when the choices are yours. Remember that good decisions come back to bless you, over and over again. Work for the ability to choose wisely…"

Douglas Pagels

"You came near when I called you, and you said, 'Do not fear.' O Lord, you took up my case; you redeemed my life."

Lamentations 3:57-58

SUNDAY, DECEMBER 9 WAS EXACTLY TWO days into my wife's postpartum period—a period in which the newborn baby gets the opportunity to be breastfed for the first time, gets easy access to mother, is given postnatal care and also the much needed nurture, cuddle and inspiration. My wife, being a first time mother, was supposed to be having an entirely new experience during this time. Experts say that a postpartum period in most cases ends during the sixth week after delivery. The only taste she had of this experience was on the day following childbirth. So, the first loss was the lack of her experience of postpartum bonding with our child. She would have no story to tell anyone about it, as many other mothers do. The experience of the early morning hours of Saturday—day one—took that experience away from her.

I now know what happened to my wife on that ill-fated day of Saturday, December 8th. It was blood clots. But, this is only a fraction of what I have learned on the journey I had begun, having no idea where I was headed. Day two fell on a Sunday. Sunday was normally our regular church day. I had planned to go to church on this day to thank God for our newborn baby, but, as it turned out, I found myself in an eight by ten feet ICU 2600 Level room, sitting by my wife pondering, worrying, terrified and bursting with anxiety. On that morning, I saw a group of doctors making rounds from one patient to another. When they got to my wife, they made a small circle, standing in front of her room, about 15 to 20 feet away. They began discussing her case, but each one of them spoke with very tight lips so that I couldn't hear what they were saying from where I was sitting. *Such secretive discussions could only be implicating something important,* I mumbled to myself. But I also thought it was a norm within the hospital setting for doctors to do what they were doing that morning.

After about five minutes they dispersed to another area; to my surprise no one said anything to me. That gave me some concern. *When people talk in such hushed tones to the exclusion of others around them, especially to the exclusion of those who need to know, it must be that the news is not good enough to share or that the need to share had not arisen,* I murmured again. As I saw the situation, it required some composure, but I was very anxious to know my wife's condition. I wanted the doctors to tell me something to keep me strong, but that didn't happen that day.

Later that day, it transpired from all the whispers around the ICU among the doctors and nurses that my wife had crossed the most crucial moment. As one doctor told me later, they believed from experience that surviving such a pulmonary embolism hinged upon the first few hours of the attack. He added that the possibility of any major changes could not be ruled out as yet. It was also said that surviving immediate death does not guarantee normalcy. In fact one report from a generalized assessment completed earlier showed that my wife had sustained an anoxic brain injury, meaning that with the brain injury comes the possibility of a seizure which would be an additional burden in her already semi-survival condition.

Inasmuch as I tried to keep a blind eye to the gloomy prognosis and espouse a positive view, I was still being haunted by the cynicism that accompanied the story of survival that was lingering around the place; I wasn't too sure my wife would make it. She was still not showing any sign of movement. All I could see were strings of tubes hanging all over her body—some for breathing, others for feeding and the rest for medications. What was the indication? I began asking myself again. She was heavily relying on the machines for survival. *It would be difficult to believe any story of hope for survival, looking at her weary condition that tells all,* again I mumbled to myself.

As noted, this was just a fraction of the gloom I would have to deal with as the story unfolded. Later, I would hear another story in an indirect way, perhaps for fear that if I were told directly, the hospital management would have to deal with two patients: a wife who was already a patient and the husband who would become a second patient on cardiac arrest. But that would not be the final number of patients. In addition there would also be the newly born baby waiting to be discharged into the hands of hospital officials. That information dampened my spirit even more deeply and the hope for survival would be forgotten for quite a while. My condition was already weakened and fraught with fear; I was flammable and ready to explode. Thankfully, it didn't happen that way. I believe it was God who redirected the situation.

Reality stared me in the face each moment. There was no way of escaping it. Given my agonizing condition I wanted some euphemism from anyone who would choose to educate me regarding the danger of blood clots in the lungs. But I guess rooted in their professional life, doctors or nurses must tell the truth as it is. Blood clots in the lungs, I was told, often lead to a critical path that continues to a bitter and sometimes deadly end.

A doctor told us in one of our discussions that the development of blood clots, a process called thrombosis within blood vessels, can lead to serious complications or death, if not detected and treated effectively and in a timely manner. He went on to say, "Those who are more likely to be affected include: sick patients, hospitalized patients, patients undergoing major surgery and patients with serious medical conditions, such as heart disease, cancer or stroke." According to him, the formation of a blood clot called deep vein thrombosis, is in itself not life threatening, but could potentially lead to high blood pressure in the vein. He added that about 10 to 20 percent of patients with DVT, who are not treated for it, develop pulmonary emboli.

Understanding all of this and having to deal with what had already occurred, re-examining the story and trying to discern how this could have been prevented, was not as important as the desire to see my wife recovered. Time was running out. We were deeply into the evening hours of the second day. I had not heard from my in-laws. They only spoke with Pastor Bernard Zougouri in Atlanta, Georgia. The deteriorating situation was persisting as the day wound down. I thought it wise to invite a family member to be with me. Pastor Zougouri was the closest I could call on, so I asked him to come down to Johnson City if he could. He agreed and came along with his wife.

Earlier that day, I had decided to go on a fast and prayer marathon, a decision I thought was much better than to keep watching the doctors congregating every morning speaking in low tones out of my range of hearing while I would be trying to guess their words.

In planning a period of fast and prayer, I didn't mention to God a specific date to end it; all I decided was that given the gravity of the situation I was going to do this until the Lord would answer my prayer—it was an open-ended fast and prayer session beginning that Sunday. About 11 P.M. that evening Pastor Zougouri and his wife Isa arrived. I was greatly touched. Although my preacher and others had come around that day, the couple's presence meant that there were now not only people who would pray with me, but they were also relatives, and they would see and explain the story clearly to my wife's parents.

Fifteen minutes after their arrival, Pastor Zougouri called Africa to inform my wife's parents that they had arrived and that we had begun to pray. In his response, that shocked me, my wife's dad told him that we had prayed and petitioned enough; it was about time to thank God and not to keep asking for help. This required faith, faith at its testing time, and was something I could not do. But as a preacher my wife's dad was doing what he knew best and had practiced for a long time. Weighing my level of faith against this, I thought my faith was nowhere near an average level. It was a time when tears were still rolling down my cheeks; I was confused and thought that my world had come to an end.

DECEMBER 10th
DAY 3
FAST AND PRAYER CONTINUED

"The Lord is near to all who call on him, to all who call on him in truth. He fulfills the desires of those who fear him; he hears their cry and saves them."

Psalm 145:18-19

"Much outcry, little outcome."

Aesop

I HAD GONE WITHOUT FOOD FOR THE FIRST two days of my wife's incident. I won't count the first day as part of my fast and prayers. It was a day of absolute chaos. Totally confused, I had no sense of order and organization; hence seeking a solution through prayers was out of the question on day one. I was certainly in a state of despair and found no meaning to life. Having prayed with my wife for days, weeks, months and years for a child, to see our effort and joy turned into a nightmare in the twinkle of an eye was discouraging and unbelievable.

As noted, by the close of day two, reality began sinking in; my eyes could now clearly see and the mind believed that indeed the woman that lay before me in complete silence was my wife. It was about time to be a man, because in truth, "Much outcry produces only little outcome." So, the decision to take the incident to a whole new level was necessary. That was when I began developing some coping mechanisms. I decided to continue my fast and prayer with some maturity for as long as it would take for my wife to respond to treatment.

On that day, the exam that was performed that morning showed some ambivalent results. The examiner pointed out that "Despite the somewhat limited opacification of the pulmonary arteries, there was a large pulmonary embolism extending from the right main pulmonary artery into all segments of the right, middle and lower lobes." The examiner suspected there were right upper lobe pulmonary emboli, but believed they were not well defined. The good news, however, was that her lungs were cleared of clots. Even though she had shown no discernable movement to indicate any sign of recovery, the fact that her lungs were clear and her breath level was between 25 to 35 percent caused me to become confident enough to build my faith upon this as I continued my marathon of fast and prayer.

Such a generalized assessment report was not good enough to maintain my strength, but as a believer, I regrouped my mind and continued to fast and pray. I hoped that my wife would gradually recover.

Faith was the bedrock of my confidence, but it was assaulted by the fact that my life had detoured so dramatically; however, it was a force capable of thrusting me through the many unknown difficult days ahead. In such desperation for my wife's speedy recovery, I could only reduce my stress level if I abided in the truth found in the word of God. To do so, the challenge was to ignore human or professional reality evidenced by my wife's unconsciousness. There was another reality I had to contend with. My newly born baby was still at the hospital and his discharge was overdue. The hospital management had called me to a meeting and I had started to search for someone to take him home for me. In these circumstances, the most likely outcome would probably be some professional counseling. While it is true that professional counseling is the mental panacea of our modern world, in this crisis I chose to go directly to the Chief Counselor and Healer of all mankind, our Lord and Savior, Jesus Christ.

In Jeremiah 33:3, the Lord says, *"Call to me and I will answer you and tell you great and unsearchable things you do not know."* Also, in John 10:27-29, Jesus says, *"My sheep listen to my voice; I know them, and they follow me. I give them eternal life, and they shall never perish; no one can snatch them out of my father's hand."* These scriptures provide assurances, protections and a sense of awareness that the Lord is always present with us, even in our darkest period. They became the core of my self-coping skills as I embarked upon the next phase of my troubles, trials and tribulations.

While my fast and prayer were in full force on that day, I was still haunted by a sense of fear and failure. I had fasted and prayed before, also with my wife. In those earlier days we fasted and prayed for things many would say are everyday petitions to God. For example, we prayed for a job in times of joblessness, for a safe journey when traveling, for strength where there were weaknesses and for children where barrenness seemed to be present. In this session I was praying for God to raise up someone whom many, including the doctors, had concluded would not survive. In other words, I was attempting an uphill task—something I had not done before—praying to raise up someone who was clinically dead or, as rumors had it, was dead. But because it was an extreme situation, I thought it also required extreme measures since I did not have the faith of Jesus who raised Lazarus from the dead. My approach was to keep going until the Lord would hear me and so, I embraced a journey with no end in sight.

The book of Matthew talks about the manner of fast and prayer. It says in chapter 6:16-18, *"Moreover, when ye fast, be not as the hypocrites, of a sad countenance. For they disfigure their faces that they may appear to men to fast, verily I say unto you, they have their reward; but thou, when thou fastest, anoint thine head, and wash thou face; that thou appear not unto men to fast, but unto thou father which is in secret, and thou father who seeth in secret, shall reward thee openly."* This was another task for me. I was already distant from everything around me. Would it be possible for me not to be seen as a wan person? Also, friends and church members had been coming around offering me food to eat and I had refused, giving reasons based on lies, saying that I had had something already, thank you. These were all temptations that started on the first day of my fast and prayer and continued to torment me.

What this means is that for a fast and prayer to be conducted free of temptations, one must be secluded. That way ensures even more time with God and a time to meditate. In my case, I couldn't leave my wife alone at the hospital. I felt it would be a breach of our vow—"for better and for worse." I also wanted to be near her to see everything for myself and didn't want to be told anything second-hand. But again, despite all of these temptations, I knew I would only be successful if I trusted the grace of God to carry me through and not depended solely on my faith or righteousness. So, day three gave me an idea of what to expect as I attempted to challenge the unseen enemy who goes around looking for someone to devour.

DECEMBER 11th
DAY 4
BRAIN SCAN

"I wish a lot of things, I wish that life was like the movies are."

Sir Alan Herbert

"It is easy for men to talk one thing and think another."

Publilius Syrus

MY FAST AND PRAYER CONTINUED ON the third day as planned. As anyone would expect with such an unstable situation at hand, the possibility of strange things happening at any moment to taint a spiritual moment and bring it to an arbitrary end was inevitable. I looked forward to seeing the doctors in the morning even if they didn't include me in their discussions; I wanted to get a hint of the outcome from any test done during the day. But I was fortunate to always have someone to keep me abreast with developments as they occurred. It was about noon when sitting by my wife's bedside, one of the nurses came to me and told me that the brain scan performed earlier did not give reason for hope. As she put it, "Everything seems to be leveled out." I asked, "What does that mean?" She said, "It isn't a good sign, but the doctors said they would do the test again."

I left the nurse and went back to my seat bewildered. Indeed, Sir Alan Herbert had it right. At that moment I truly wished that the entire incident were a movie and not an actual situation. Having facts or what people thought were the facts thrown in my face as they happened, I wasn't too sure that my fast and prayer would survive the day. If this were a movie, I would have had a choice to get out of the theater if I didn't like the show, but here I was within a real life situation. It was easy for me to plan a marathon of fast and prayer, but it had been difficult so far for me to hear these stories of dismay.

Despite this discouraging news, I held firmly to my faith, not only doubting the nurse's explanation but also rebuking it in Jesus' name and believing that what she had said was only based on human observation and that there was no speck of truth in it. That moment was a moment of faith; I guess I was ready to go to heaven at that time if Jesus were to appear before me. The moment would be short-lived and ended as soon as I went back to my wife's bedside. Like Peter whose ship was tossed by the waves of the sea when he saw Jesus and with belief stepped forth onto the water in an attempt to walk on the water like Jesus had, but momentarily began to sink, I could not hold onto my faith as I returned to the room. In the room, I began praying, refuting the nurse's statement, saying "In Jesus' name, in Jesus' name, I rebuke every attempt of the devil to sentence my wife to death." These and many other words were mentioned, but my search for instant gratification could not prevail. My wife was still hushed between life and death. She still showed no sign of life.

I sneaked into retrospection: it started with high blood pressure; she was placed on the high-risk list, then preeclampsia and blood clots ensued, and now the brain scan showed no activity. Bringing these facts into consideration, I began to believe the nurse's explanation suggesting that my wife would not survive her weakened condition.

What the nurse had told me was just the first of many reports I would receive from the doctors. It became a routine that every morning they would do a test and, based on the result, some medications would be added or subtracted and also the mode of treatment going forward would be determined. The routine began with a team of doctors and nurses congregating before the nursing station every morning.

Before the close of that day, I made up my mind never again to ask the nurse or a doctor about the result of a test. The only thing I thought was right to do henceforth was to continue my fast and prayer. Usually during the evening time, from about 10 to 11 P.M., I would receive a call from Atlanta, Georgia from Pastor Zougouri asking for a daily report. He would then call Burkina Faso to relay the news to my in-laws. That day when he called, from my tone of voice he knew things were still not well. He asked if I wanted him to come down and I said no, and I did so on two grounds. First, he had been on the road a lot, leaving his job to drive 800 miles back and forth from Atlanta. At one point, State Troopers had pulled him over and gave him a two hundred dollar ticket. I became really concerned about what he was going through for my sake. Second, once I had chosen to focus on my fast and prayer, I needed to be strong and act in a faithful way. He encouraged me saying, "We are keeping you in our prayers, don't worry, God will take care of your wife."

The scripture says in Psalm 55:22: *"Cast your cares to the Lord and he will sustain you; he will never let the righteous fall."* And in Jeremiah 29:11, it says: *"'I know the plans I have for you,' declares the Lord, 'plans to prosper you and not to harm you, plans to give you hope and a future.'"* The Lord never lies and His words are true. He is a God who fulfills His promises. I entrusted my wife's burdens to Him and I knew He would carry them for me. I ended the day with my eyes on the Lord, wishing only for the survival of my wife, without any wavering of my faith. As I tilted back in my recliner by her bedside that night, hoping and believing in my heart, I prayed that the next day would bring good tidings.

DECEMBER 12th
DAY 5
NURSE'S EFFECT

"Jesus said, 'Watch and pray so that you will not fall into temptation. The spirit is willing, but the body is weak.'"

Matthew 26:41

"Be self-controlled and alert. Your enemy the devil prowls around like a roaring lion looking for someone to devour."

1 Peter 5:8

MY WIFE'S ADMISSION RECORDS SHOW that I was the only one authorized to receive her hospital information. I was the only one that accompanied her on that day on December 6th, 2007. When she fell due to blood clots on the 8th and on the days following at the ICU 2600 Level, many friends, church members and relatives came around to sympathize. As close as I was to many of them, I did not authorize the release of any information, verbal or written, about my wife to any of them. I asked those who wanted to help me only to stay with her if I had to go on an errand outside of the hospital building. It is one thing to be of assistance and to sit with a sick person and quite another to be authorized to see the person's records.

Day five reminded me of the lesson concerning temptation when Jesus warned the disciples to watch and pray so that they might not fall into temptation. On that day I was also taught a lesson of self-control. The scripture warns us to be self-controlled and alert, that the enemy the devil prowls around like a roaring lion, looking for someone to consume.

Entering day five, my wife had not made any significant progress from the previous day. My eyes had been set on all the computer monitors, checking on everything throughout the night, from blood pressure to the ventilator, watching for signs of improvement as each monitor showed what was going on. While I waited for the result that morning after another series of tests, I had to leave for a while to check on my baby at the Labor and Delivery Ward where he was still held awaiting discharge. Just then, one of our family friends, Younger Duanah, came in. She had been there with me from the beginning. I asked her to stay with my wife until my return. She agreed and I left.

While I was away, two people came in—my brother, Michael Quewea and another friend, John Kollie. It was about noon when I got back and encountered three persons in the room with my wife. Two of them—my brother, Michael Quewea, and Younger Duanah—could not look me in the eyes. I tried asking what was going on; they gave me evasive answers. I was greatly concerned and probed further, rephrasing my question. I noticed that Younger Duanah and my brother appeared to be very sad. The redness of their eyes told me that perhaps they had been crying. *If so, what had happened in my absence?* I asked myself.

Indeed, they were crying. My friend, John Kollie told me the whole story. According to him, a nurse I will identify as only "the one with blonde hair" came into Daniella's room to administer medications; when they asked how my wife was doing, she told them that she was not sure that my wife would improve. At that time D.Q. was showing no significant movement of any kind. The nurse also told them that going into a fifth day without improvement indicated that she might not survive. Such information spoken so haphazardly could be heartbreaking to anyone. It made me angry on many levels. I thought the nurse's behavior raised a number of questions: Was she respecting the patient's rights? Who gave her the authority to speak out of turn? In fact, what was the demarcation between what should be said to visitors about a patient and what should not?

The situation caused me to lose my composure. Here I was fasting and praying, trying to avoid temptation, but having no way to escape it. It wasn't only about temptation. It also confirmed my skepticism about the level of secrecy the doctors maintained following the meetings they held each morning. I became furious at one thing—the breach of confidence. I felt that the nurse had gone too far; she had violated my wife's privacy.

I was told that my friend John Kollie, a very committed Christian in my view, had taken a leap of faith. He had rebuked the nurse, telling her she was not a god to be able to foretell someone's destiny and that my wife would rise up from that hospital bed without any ill effect. I realized later that it was the same nurse who had told me the brain scan showed no activity—that everything had seemed to be leveled out, as she described it. It was a day that started on the wrong footing, so I decided to find a solution that would prevent such future occurrences.

I tried to hold my peace, since I was still fasting and praying. Coincidentally, at the same time one of my church brothers, Kent, who is usually a very jovial man, arrived. I seized the opportunity to explain the story to him. He knew how angry I was, so he decided to privately go and see the nurse and other hospital employees in the area. After several minutes of talks behind closed doors, he came back with assurances that everything was under control. I was thankful to him for helping me to avoid confusion since I was committing my wife's care into the hands of the Lord through fast and prayer. I viewed this incident, like others mentioned, as temptation. I knew the devil was at work because he was being battled against. But again, the Lord is always faithful. In Hebrews 2:18, the scripture says: *"Because Christ himself suffered when he was tempted, he is able to help those who are being tested."* Also, in 1 Corinthians 10:13, the scripture says: *"No temptation has seized you except what is common to man. And God is faithful; he will not let you be tempted beyond what you can bear. But when you are tempted he will also provide a way out so that you can stand up under it."* I believe Brother Kent was sent on this day as a conduit for the work of the Lord to be realized.

DECEMBER 13th
DAY 6
BODY MOVEMENT

"'I have seen His ways, but I will heal him; I will guide him and restore comfort to him, creating praise on the lips of the mourners in Israel. Peace, peace, to those far and near,' says the Lord. 'And I will heal them.'"

Isaiah 57:18-19

"Praise be to the God and Father of our Lord Jesus Christ, the Father of compassion and the God of all comfort, who comforts us in all our troubles, so that we can comfort those in any trouble with the comfort we ourselves have received from God."

2 Corinthians 1:3-4

DAY SIX BROUGHT SOME COMFORT; it began on a promising footing compared to previous days. My wife was quite calm and appeared to be more relaxed. However, reports obtained from her generalized assessment done early that day showed a number of contrasting findings. At about 6 A.M. she was taken off sedation but was still incubated, non-responsive to verbal commands and her eyes were still closed. Her blood pressure was okay to start with, but later, at about 10 A.M., it went up to 150/80 with a temperature of 100 degrees. The doctors were still making an effort to clear the clots from her lungs, while at the same time they had to deal with the blood pressure and keep a close watch over the incision for possible bleeding. The observation made about noon on that day convinced the doctors that she was still critically ill, as she was being heavily medicated without much progress by day six.

I was still holding on to my fast and prayer, hoping that all would be well by His grace. Sitting by the bed of my wife who was at the time a critically ill patient who showed no sign of improvement, I was unexpectedly shocked by what I saw. It was about 5 P.M. and I was sitting in my usual seat near her bed, quietly pondering the situation, when, for the first time in six days, I noticed a movement in her body. It was beyond my imagination. I tried to contain my emotion to avoid others from noticing my feelings and kept a close watch to see if there would be another sign before uttering a word. It happened again and again. But because the atmosphere had been extremely tense with many believing that she was still critically ill, I did not want to be seen faking any improvement. So, I still kept my lips sealed for a while, watching for more signs.

In order to know whether or not she was making real movements, I thought of speaking to her to see if she could respond. That way, I would have the evidence to prove my case. So I said, "D.Q.," as I usually prefer to call her, "do you know where you are?" She did not answer. I followed up this time with a statement instead of a question. "You've been here at ICU since December 8th, and your baby John is still at the Labor and Delivery Ward, yet to be discharged." I finally asked her, "Do you want me to bring him to you?" There was still no response.

I was doing all the talking, believing that she was hearing me but unable to talk. In the end, I felt she had made enough movement to prove to me that she would respond if I brought the baby in, so I went to one of the nurses to tell her what I had experienced. Surprisingly, she told me my wife had made the same movement a few hours earlier when I was out. She then said, "Let's go and talk to her again to see if she will make a movement." This time it was the nurse asking and she asked my wife, "If you want to see your baby, wiggle your finger for me." Again my wife wiggled her finger. The nurse was delighted to see that. At this juncture I wish for you, the reader, to empathize with me for a moment and discern what my feelings would have been like. As you can imagine, I was already about ten feet away from the nurse, running down the stairs as I was calling out to her, "I am going to get the baby, I will be back soon."

With the speed of a hurricane, in less than five minutes I was at the Labor and Delivery Ward on a journey that would have normally taken me ten minutes. Detecting a huge smile on my face, one of the nurses said, "You look okay today." I said, "Yes indeed, I am okay," and I went on to tell the story of my wife's movement and improvement. I asked the nurses if I could take the baby to my wife and see if she would show more signs of improvement. They told me that was okay, but they would come with the baby once he was dressed. I left and went back to the ICU to wait for them. While I was at the Labor and Delivery Ward, the nurse had been talking to my wife. She told me D.Q. had made more movements. I thanked God for that news as well. The baby was finally brought in and the nurse I will refer to as the "tall one," who accompanied Baby John, laid him on his mother's chest so she could feel him. At the same time they were talking to her, but surprisingly, she didn't move or talk back. It was a little discouraging to see my baby leave without hearing his mommy's voice after we had tried everything we could think of. So far his only postpartum experience with his mom had been on December 7th. Not enough by all accounts.

Later, the doctors told me that her body movement was non-purposeful and that it was only a sign that her body was recovering from the heavily sedated stage. I became even more edgy as the day gradually entered into the evening hours. By 8 P.M. she was given her evening medications. Wondering how to end the day on a positive note, I thought of doing something that my wife could respond to. Talking wasn't helping, even if I shook her to get her attention. At times I would turn her, move her legs here and there as though I was helping to reposition her, even though she wasn't moving. But I only pretended to do that, so that when the nurses would catch me, they might think I was only helping them do their job.

I tried to figure out strategies to get my wife's attention. Shouting was out of the question; in fact that could have led the nurses to admitting me to a psychiatric center due to unusual behavior. Everything I attempted didn't make sense or could not work. I would be surprised later by what took place. After minutes of fruitless effort to come up with some new idea, I went to the restroom to relieve myself. Most toilets at the hospital are not like those in homes—they flush very loudly. I didn't know this. When I was done and was talking to myself about what I could come up with, I flushed the toilet as I stepped out. The sound was so loud that I thought I had broken something, but at the same time I saw that my wife had moved her leg very forcefully, to the point that I had to reposition it back on the bed. The noise from the flushing of the commode scared me but the reaction from my wife created some joy by surprise. The joy was that she was alive; the surprise was that she had the ability to move and I was also scared because she almost fell off the bed. *What a coincidence,* I sighed. Under normal circumstances, I would be sorry that I had disturbed her sleep, but on this occasion I was happy because this was how I wanted to end my day. I remained tongue-tied on this one, keeping it as a secret and something to do whenever the doctors would come with their stories about non-purposeful movement. For the rest of the night, I guess I flushed that toilet more than a hundred times, just trying to keep my wife stimulated. It worked, but I am sorry I did that. Of course, flushing the toilet was not a way to find a solution. The fact that I was willing to deal with the problem to the very end through fast and prayers could be, and I was thankful to God for the endurance and strength.

DECEMBER 14ᵗʰ
DAY 7
BREATHING IMPROVEMENT

"You hear, O Lord, the desire of the afflicted; you encourage them, and you listen to their cry."

Psalm 10:17

THROUGHOUT THE FIRST SEVEN DAYS OF our saga of slow progress towards resuscitation, my confidence level was measurable following the rise and fall of hope on a number of occasions. I was now confident that time actually couldn't take away anything that had already been given. And that was the life of my wife that the blood clots had brought into suspension during these past days. She was my treasure in years gone by, and still is mine to keep for endless numbers of years to come. It was encouraging to see another sign of life on this day—the improvement in her breathing. The Lord is gracious and deserves our praises.

My wife was mildly sedated on this day and was able to respond to painful stimuli to a visible extent. The team of doctors and nurses at ICU 2600 Level were still continuing their good work to ensure her recovery, given the improvement they had sensed. Ironically, her mildly sedated condition was creating some problems. There were a lot of movements of the hands and feet. The nurses had to restrain her to protect her from a fall and also to ensure that the tubes attached to her would not become detached.

The day itself was similar to the previous days. Each morning between 6 and about 9 A.M. a team of doctors and nurses would routinely stop by to read the report from the night nurses and make assessments and recommendations as to the next course of action. They would then hold a meeting, usually in front of the patient's door, just a few feet away, and stand in a circle. That day, as on many other days, it started on a good note with the movements that were now called purposeful movements my wife was making. These movements said a lot about how far the journey had brought us and what our expectations should be for the days ahead of us.

My wife was still on a ventilator, even though her movements had given me a deep sigh of relief. She had to be on the ventilator due to respiratory insufficiency. The obvious question was, if the movements continued, how long would she take to be able to breathe on her own without the respirator? On the other hand, considering what had gone on during the previous six days, I had to be thankful and needed to avoid a lot of wishful thinking. The day was a day of a lot of improvements. Later, at about 1 P.M., the readings on the ventilator showed an improvement in her breathing. I went out to call the nurse to be double sure of what I was looking at. She confirmed that my wife was breathing a little above the level induced by the machine. The nurse looked at me and smiled and said, "Good news." Before leaving she said, "If this continues for the rest of the day, we might remove the ventilator to observe how much she can do on her own." Indeed, it was good news, but I didn't want to rush the removal of the tube.

Day seven reminded me of my wife's famous quote: "God's blessings are not followed by sorrows." I couldn't agree more with this. We now had a baby, the outcome of our many years of fast and prayers. In my prayers and thanksgiving on this day I poured my heart out before God, as though He were visibly sitting before me. I said, "Lord, this is what your daughter used to say and believe about your work; are you going to prove her wrong?" I would continue my prayer by telling God to continue His good work and to demonstrate to man that His miracles still exist. "Do it and do it now," I would continue in my prayers. "Father, if you will let this pass and give me my wife back from the shackles of the enemies, I will magnify your name; I will praise you at all times…"

I was convinced that day seven was a moment to seize and take advantage of in prayers and rededication. Doubts, unbelief, fatigue in faith had all clouded my mind on the first few days. And like Job, sometimes in my mind I would ask whether or not there was any meaning to life after investing one's time and effort in developing and nurturing a relationship to see it expire like a vapor being washed away into thin air.

With a dash of frenzy, humor and dedication combined, that day I prayed like never before. I guess my prayerful spirit on that day could be best described as the "last chance my wife had to survive."

The desire to see my wife survive was extremely strong. The level of intensity in my prayers was also enhanced, but when viewed critically, the idea of unbelief appeared to also be inherent. My actions were like that of Thomas, one of Jesus' disciples. When the Lord was crucified, He ascended to heaven and afterward, when He appeared to His disciples on His return, everyone believed He was the Lord, except Thomas. Thomas said, "If you are truly the One, show me the palm of your hands and let me see where the nails had been drilled into them." Jesus did so to convince him. My anxiousness to see my wife out of the hospital perhaps blinded me from seeing the evidence that the Lord had started his work on my wife. It was obvious from the fact that she had improved so well on a single day, day seven, and from the way that it happened; my thousands of words of prayers were not what the Lord needed.

When the Lord is ready to answer prayers, it is not based on our righteousness or how much we impress Him with our descriptive words. When we have problems, like hunger, lack of security, grief… all He needs to do is simple, as simple as when He took five pieces of bread to feed the multitudes or when the children of Israel were redeemed from captivity in Egypt by the rod He gave to Moses to split the sea and create a route to safety.

The Psalmist says, *"Because he loves me, I will rescue him; I will protect him; for He acknowledges my name. He will call upon me, and I will answer him; I will be with him in trouble, I will deliver him and honor him"* (Psalm 91:14-15). The Bible teaches that a fervent prayer of a righteous man avails much. Thankfully, I would learn later about miracles similar to those that Jesus performed in those days, as my wife's recovery unfolded right before my watchful eyes.

Finally, they reached a decision for a transfer to ICU 2700 Level. When asked why she was being removed, one of the nurses told me that ICU 2600 Level dealt with severe cases and that it was only a holding place for patients coming out of surgery.

So, I was glad to hear the nurse's explanation that only patients in critical condition were kept at ICU 2600 Level. What that suggested to me was that my wife was recuperating from a critical condition to a much better level of health. In my brief conversation with the nurse prior to our journey to ICU 2700, I was reminded of the possibility to remove her breathing tube during her stay at ICU 2700. Of course, I had been ambivalent about this, but I accepted her suggestion and was looking forward to seeing the day the decision would be made to remove the tube.

DECEMBER 15th
DAY 8
INTENSIVE CARE UNIT 2700

"This I called to mind and therefore I have hope: because of the Lord's great love, we are not consumed, for his compassion never fails."

Lamentations 3: 21-23

"The prayer, offered in faith, will make the sick person well; the Lord will raise him up. If he had sinned, he will be forgiven… confess your sins to each other and pray for each other so that you may be healed. The prayer of a righteous man is powerful and effective."

James 5:15-16

THE SCRIPTURES ABOVE DESCRIBE MY feelings perfectly as day eight approached and as I looked back on what the Lord had done, especially on day seven. I felt it was due to the great love and compassion that the Lord has for us, and the sense of empathy for those with great affliction and burdens. I had always refused to tell people how faithful I am. To proclaim faithfulness one must take several things into consideration. Even Peter, as I have repeatedly mentioned in this book, a man who lived and worked with Jesus, could not hold onto his faith when he saw the wave of the sea approaching, even though he had asked the Lord for permission and was encouraged to do what he wanted (i.e. walk on water).

As humans we can be easily overcome and unless we invoke the Lord's protection and guidance, we may be doomed and defeated by our enemies. I had always felt it was not through work or faith but rather by His grace that everything I had asked of the Lord was given to me. But what I could confidently say, especially during this time, was that I was a prayerful man, a guy who wanted to be at the feet of the Lord begging Him for mercy until He would bring my wife back to life. Sometimes, even while praying, I felt some weaknesses, but in every journey, the first step is always the most important one. I took it one day at a time.

While it was true that on reaching day eight there were some improvements, each day had not passed by without some form of setback as well. We were taking two steps forward and one step backward. In some cases it was the reverse—one step forward, two steps back. In fact, nurses confirmed that such a condition required that kind of recovery level. So, on day eight, my wife's condition appeared a bit hopeless again. Based on her assessment report that morning, it was said that her condition was still critical. She was still on full ventilator support, unresponsive to verbal commands. But there was always some good news. The good news was, her eyes had spontaneously opened, which gave me some hope. The fluctuating blood pressure was 143/80 on that day.

At the pace she was going after eight days of treatment, it would take a big heart to believe that survival was possible; it would take the kind of faith that moves mountains and perhaps it would require a prophet to predict the future. Perhaps I was the only one living in my own world, still believing there was hope for survival. I was in the middle of it all—caught between the doctors' report and my wife's actual response to treatment, as I continued to observe it on a daily basis when I was with her by myself in the room. Those reports that I received each day and the constant reminder that she was still in a critical condition began taking a toll on me. But my strength at that time was drawn from God's promises and from those around me, like my church members, community members and relatives of my wife. I remember during that day a call came from Atlanta, Georgia from Pastor Zougouri. According to him, he had just completed a long discussion with my father-in-law in Africa who was planning to come to Johnson City. He had told Pastor Zougouri to tell me that I should not worry, that they were with me in prayers and that I was like a son to them. I could not appreciate his kindness more. That message encouraged me even more to remain prayerful until my wife would get better.

From day one to this point, I had entrusted my wife's survival to science as expressed in medicine and to prayer and my trust in God. But as you can see, medical doctors had given up. They gave me a reason to believe that there was only so much they could do for my wife. What was left to complete the healing process was beyond their competence. Simply put, where the knowledge of man ends, the work of the Lord begins to enhance the ability of man. Because of what appeared to be faithlessness in the attitudes of some of those nurses and doctors, I had every reason to glorify the Lord, but at the same time I appreciated what they had done. Their early intervention up to this day was perhaps the limit of their strength. They had already demonstrated their shortcomings right from day one when it was rumored that my wife was dead and during the encounter my friends had with the nurse, as well as other instances mentioned before. I didn't think that any human had the answers to the question regarding what should have happened next. It was at this juncture that my prayers became stronger and I chose to remain with the only weapon that was left—my prayers.

Several others joined me in prayer: members of the Central Church of Christ, the Centre d'Evangelisation International Tabernacle Bethel Israel Church where my father-in-law preaches, some friends and others.

Along with prayers was hope, hope that as I prayed, the Lord would listen to me and answer me. The scripture says, *"The Lord delights in those who fear him, who put their hope in his unfailing love"* (Psalms 147:11). As a Christian, my hope in the Lord gave me the courage to be optimistic within my dilemma. The Psalmist asks, *"Why are you downcast, O my soul? Why so disturbed within me? Put your hope in God, for I will yet praise him, my savior and my God"* (Psalm 42:5). So, with the depression that appeared on day eight again, as much as I was shaken in my faith, so was I strengthened by my hope in God. Based on my prayers and the prayers of others, I was hoping that His unfailing love and grace were powerful enough to give me courage to continue to live in my own world, still believing that the Lord was on my side.

As the day came to an end with more and more friends, relatives and church members pouring in, in sympathetic response to the worsening situation, I was touched by the outpouring of love and concerns. It also made me feel that in a time of crisis, those who show up to greet you are people to remember when the crisis is over. As noted, they helped us in many ways. Some came with encouragement, some were there to assist in areas where we were lacking and yet others were there to see it to the end. They made us feel that our problem was also their problem. These were people who truly understood that the life we live is symbiotic. As a friend once said, "One hand washes another." This goes to confirm the power of social sensitivities and social connections. For the rest of the night, my wife slept soundly until the next day.

DECEMBER 16th
DAY 9
ATTEMPT TO REMOVE BREATHING TUBE

"Jesus told him, 'because you have seen me, you have believed; blessed are those who have not seen yet believed.'"

John 20:29

"Jesus said to her, 'I am the resurrection and the life, he who believes in me will live, even though he dies; and whoever lives and believes in me will never die.'"

John 11:25-26

ONE WAY OF PROVING THAT SOMETHING really exists is to see it. Many times we hear people say, "Seeing is believing." On day nine, my faith was tested and I failed the test. Actually that was one of my many failures based on fear. The book of Hebrews defines faith as *"the substance of things hoped for, the evidence of things not seen"* (Heb. 11:1). My faith was as strong as it could get on the morning of day nine. It was due to my belief that my wife had crossed past the danger zone. Her breathing had improved so well that I strongly believed that she could survive without the breathing tube. When the nurses approached me that morning to say that by midday they would remove the breathing tube, I winced. I told them no, not yet, she needs a little more time. Well, from the medical standpoint they knew better than I did. I guess they were surprised by my reaction, but as a husband, it was my right to suggest what I thought was good for my wife.

Minutes after my initial disagreement, I detected a thought within my subconscious mind, *"You have wrecked your faith in God."* I was in deep fear and realized that my faith had been suspended as I clung onto apprehension. While I was sorry towards God for being faithless, I also believe that this was the human side that every one of us expresses. When our faith is tested, we back out. Abraham did it when he denied Sarah to be his wife, and Peter did it also when he was sinking into the waters and cried out unto Jesus for rescue.

As humans, the slightest chaos shakes our faith. Again, this is why I am careful not to proclaim faithfulness. For me, it is work in progress. Removing the tube meant a lot to me. It was a breathing aid to my wife. I wasn't too sure what the outcome would be when they removed it. Would it be the end of life or would they be fast enough to reconnect the tube to avoid any catastrophe if needed? How much could she do on her own or how long could she go without the aid of the tube? Although I was at the prime time of my fast and prayer marathon, those difficult questions could not leave me alone. Regardless of the fast and prayer, in my mind I was saying things like, *"God said we should be wise,"* and *"A fool dies many times before his time."* I was simply feeding fear and negativity into my mind every second of my contemplation.

My fear had convinced me that one more day of prayer with my father-in-law would create better timing to remove the tube. I had learned that he would be arriving soon in Atlanta, Georgia where he was due to spend a day at a church conference. The surprising thing was, the main doctors who were going to remove the tube had not arrived. Those I talked with were the nurses who were sent to prepare me. So, even though I had said no, it didn't mean anything until the doctors were consulted.

When the team of doctors arrived that morning, they noticed that my wife's eyes were open, so they tried some verbal prompts, but she couldn't follow their instructions; she did, however, turn towards the direction of the noise. I guess the toilet flushing that I had performed several times back at ICU 2600 was instructional enough that she hadn't forgotten that. Her blood pressure was 148/88 and her temperature was 91. They also checked the incision and found it to be intact. Her respiratory status had improved again and was far better than on the previous days. The doctors were convinced that her breathing was beyond the level of the machine and that it was okay to give her a test by removing the tube. I asked one of the doctors what would happen if she failed the breathing test. She said, "That's why I am here; we would put the tube back." I asked again, just to be sure, if there was any other way, apart from removing the tube completely. She gave me an answer that was much more reassuring. She said, "The tube can remain attached but we could cut the machine off so that if it became necessary, we could turn it on again."

The answer satisfied me but I was not completely convinced to let it happen. Two of my church members were with me that morning. They all tried to convince me but they realized that I wasn't giving up my fear. I told them that my wife's dad would be arriving the next day and I would like him to be there before that was done. They agreed and left.

Day nine was the second day at ICU 2700, and again, considering what the nurse had said that ICU 2700 dealt with non-critical cases, I was appeased by spending the second night with my wife whose breathing continued to improve. Despite the signs of improvement, I treated each day with the same measure of strength, as though it were the only day left for survival. There was no time to celebrate, but it was important to remain resolute in my prayers and fast as I looked forward to God for nothing but total healing. At the same time, the encouraging words of my wife, "God's blessings are not followed by sorrows," continued to resonate with me. Her words never made sense to me before, but as time went on, I began to realize what she meant. They have now become a source of encouragement to me as they were to others when they came to her for counsel.

Later that day I received a message that my father-in-law had arrived in Atlanta. That night I called him to acquaint him with the details and inform him about what to expect on his arrival. He was due in Johnson City between 10 and 11 A.M. During that night many things ran through my mind, all of them negative. I had just remembered an incident that had occurred about a month before. A guy I knew was admitted to the same ICU 2700 because he had been choking. When I visited him, he was only alive thanks to a feeding tube and a breathing tube; and because the doctors knew that he could not survive without the breathing tube, they consulted with the family on the critical nature of his case. The discussion with the family members centered on the possibility of removing the breathing tube. His condition, as I remember, was as terminal as my wife's. They removed the tube and he died a few hours later. Remembering this incident, I couldn't sleep that night because my wife was due for the same process of removing the tube the following day.

There were many questions on my mind: *Lord, how are we going to cross this bridge? Will tomorrow be the last day of my wife's life? Have my many days of fast and prayers been in vain? As a man, I know I am a sinner, but won't you forgive me and spare my wife?* My questions and quarrel with God that night were more than ordinary prayers. I had slept infrequently since the blood clots, but that night surpassed the previous days. I was always on the alert. It was as if I had drunk a gallon of coffee to stay awake. I could not snooze nor close my eyes for a minute. I kept watching over my wife, fixing her bed sheet, even if it didn't need to be fixed. I was trying to do something that could change the plans to remove the tube the next day. But I really didn't know what I could do besides praying.

I spoke to my wife as though we were in conversation, even though she could not talk back. I wanted to see a miracle happen at my discretion. As she could not talk, I wanted her to show some more movement or even get up. My emotions were indescribable. The night was deepening and the day was fast approaching. There was nothing else I could do to change the order of the day. But the Word of God remained truthful—our thoughts are not His thoughts and our ways are not His ways. He does things in His own timing. That time had not arrived and I was living in the shadow of my fears. He had only given me a sense of His will by demonstrating the movements my wife had been making. Even given these signs, I was still pondering and worrying.

DECEMBER 17th
DAY 10
ARRIVAL OF FATHER-IN-LAW
BREATHING TUBE REMOVED

"Because God wanted to make the unchanging nature of His purpose very clear to the heirs of what was promised, He confirmed it with an oath. God did this so that… we who have fled to take hold of the hope offered to us may be greatly encouraged."

Hebrews 6:17-18

IT WAS THE PURPOSE OF THE LORD TO redeem my wife from the hands of the enemies, but my inability to understand His strategies in solving problems again tainted my faith. The Lord has a way of dealing with people. Because He understands all things far and near, it is always difficult for us to understand His strategies. His strategies in getting to a solution of a problem always expose our human weaknesses. When we feel the lights are about to be turned off on us, He recharges the batteries; when we think the doors are closing on us, He provides the opening. Day ten was again another example of the Lord's peculiar ways of doing things.

My memory was still fresh as to how it all happened in the early morning hours of December 8th. That fateful Saturday morning when I saw my wife become motionless, speechless and unconscious, within the twinkle of an eye, became a day I will never forget. The only last words she mentioned that morning were, "Daddy, I can't breathe" and she was gone. As I went through the countdown of the remaining hours towards the removing of the breathing tube, the thoughts of December 8th imprinted themselves upon me with perfect memory.

It was about 7:30 A.M.; the doctors were scheduled to perform the procedure at 8 A.M. That meant that if the devil was stronger than the Lord, 30 minutes was the only time I would have to see my wife at least hanging unto life. With me that morning were my father-in-law, my preacher, an elder from the church and another church brother. I appeared confident on the outside, but within me was a man still fighting to prevent the removal of the tube and asking for more days. Within me was that little man who kept reminding me that there were only a few hours left within which I would still be able to see my wife alive. When the doctors arrived, at first they did not allow any of us to enter the room with them. We were in the corridor of the building when they went in to perform the procedure. With my confused mind, I kept praying silently. The process was fast; it took about three minutes to complete. One of the doctors came out to let us know that they were done and that it was okay for us to go in.

I noticed that we were all quiet. I guess there were a lot of inner prayers going on in each of us. But later we held hands and brother Tim led us in a few words of prayer.

After the prayer, it was time to go in and see my wife. Brother Tim declined the offer to go in and the rest of us went in to see her without him. I guess seeing someone suffering was difficult for him.

We came to realize that the day was a major step forward towards my wife's recovery. But none of us, including the doctors, knew how long she could manage without the support of the oxygen tube. Whether or not it was the beginning of another period of difficulties, only time would tell. The situation caused my vigilance to increase. I felt that for the next countless number of days, I would be much closer to my wife, making sure that I would watch out for any unusual breathing problem so that I would be able to quickly report it. As for my father-in-law, only a mind reader could tell what was going on in his mind. He was so calm that no indication of depression or worry could be suspected from his body language or facial expression.

Although they had removed the tube, they had not given us any green light regarding possible improvements; they still believed that her condition was terminal. But with God on our side, my father-in-law and I were ready to go any distance. He helped to restructure our plans for care at the hospital. From day one until this day, I was going 24/7. The only time I left the hospital was to go and have a shower and then I would come back. There were also a number of my wife's family members with us. Some had arrived from Africa and others from other states here in the United States. I was getting the much-needed support morally, spiritually and even financially from others and from the Church.

By the grace of God, my wife held on pretty well during the afternoon and the evening hours of that day. By the late evening hours, they initiated more breathing treatment to help clear the air passage as she continued to breathe on her own. That night, before my father-in-law went home, we prayed for over 30 minutes. By myself during the night, I also continued to pray. The first day without the breathing tube was crucial for survival, the doctors had said. If she managed to survive this day, it would be another step toward recovery. To me, living through that day and night was like Moses leading the children of Israel across the Red Sea. We made it safely to the next day. I will always be thankful to the Lord.

DECEMBER 18th
DAY 11
BABY DISCHARGED AFTER 12 DAYS

"Nothing wastes more energy than worrying. The longer one carries a problem, the heavier it gets. Don't take things too seriously. Live a life of serenity, not a life of regrets."

Douglas Pagels

"My flesh and my heart may fail, but God is the strength of my heart and my portion forever."

Psalms 73:26

"The Lord gives strength to the weary and increases the power of the weak."

Isaiah 40: 29

AS YOU MAY KNOW BY NOW, A GREATER portion of my time was spent in inconsistency—worrying, disbelieving, then trusting… a bit of everything. I suspect the issue of worry is one thing that never goes away, especially in times of trials and tribulations. As we dip into worries directly or indirectly, in most cases the most likely outcome is depression. Pagels rightly says, *"Nothing wastes more energy than worrying, and the longer one carries a problem, the heavier it gets…"* Some of my problems were to do with my baby. I realized that the longer my baby stayed at the hospital, the more difficult this became for me. He did not stay there due to health problems; he was there because there was no one to care for him at home. Combined with the terminal illness of his mother, I was really held between two giant walls of discomfort.

For me, the immediate symptoms of discomfort or worry were the lack of appetite and weight loss. Prior to my wife's blood clots I was overweight—210 pounds at 5 feet 6 inches. When the situation began taking a toll on me, I dropped down to 145 pounds. Trying to keep me strong, some friends joked, saying, "You look good in this structure." Others said, "You have a great formula for weight loss."

For me, my body structure was sufficient to explain to God physically how dire the situation was for me. I saw it as a formula to work my way to the Lord so that He would listen to my supplications—discharging my baby from the hospital and giving my wife a speedy recovery. It was not a formula I can

41

suggest to anyone who wishes to lose weight. It was not a formula I would like to sell on eBay or to establish a reality TV show about, like many people do.

On a more serious note, worry is a cause of severe medical problems, like stress, depression and high blood pressure. In fact, as you will read in detail later, stress and tension contributed to my wife's high blood pressure before her pregnancy. All of those symptoms were the result of worries.

In Psalms 73:26, as noted above, *"My flesh and my heart fail, but God is the strength of my heart and my portion forever,"* tells me a lot about my hurtle into the problems that led me to agonize over my wife's recovery and the discharge of my baby from hospital that was long overdue. But Isaiah says it this way, *"The Lord gives strength to the weary and increases the power of the weak"* (Isaiah 40:29).

In case you have forgotten after reading the first several pages to this point, or if opening this book, and scanning through the chapters you found these daily notes about "baby finally discharged from the hospital" interesting, and chose to begin from here but are also interested why I chose those scriptures and the quote from Pagels on failure, weakness and worries, the reason is simple. By day 11, which was now December 18th, my baby had spent exactly 12 days at the hospital. When my wife gave birth on the 7th, her medical report showed that she was okay and was expected to be discharged on the following Monday, December 10th, having spent only three days after delivery in the hospital. On that very Friday of December 7th, the nurses had begun her orientation on postpartum activities, like breastfeeding and general care for the baby at home. The baby was also fine, and ready to go home with his mother. With everything set to go, the ill-fated day of Saturday aborted the plans when the blood clots manifested. The mother had to be taken elsewhere and the only choice for the baby was to remain at the Labor and Delivery Ward. Those with whom he shares his birthday and even those who were born afterwards had all been discharged while he remained at the center as the "nurses' baby." I truly appreciate the nurses' efforts and care.

Many times I was asked to take the baby home; social workers got involved, but thankfully, the hospital administration understood my plight and postponed the time to a later date of my choice. That date depended upon my in-laws who were several thousands of miles away across the ocean in Africa. There were others who were here in the US who had chosen to come but had to go through normal procedures to get time off their respective work places. While I awaited the arrival of these family members, the Labor and Delivery Center provided me with a spare room where I could spend some time with my baby during the day or early evening hours and later go back to the intensive care unit (ICU) to his mother. This became a regular routine for me. I would pick him up, take him to the room, feed him, change him and talk to him about his mother's whereabouts. I knew he could not speak back to me, but I believe he could hear me. So, Baby John, unlike many of his peers, spent part of his crucial postpartum period in the arms of the nurses. Again, I am thankful to the hospital administration for stepping in and also thankful to all the nurses who helped me in my time of need.

Finally, members of my wife's family arrived and day 11 was designated as the time to discharge Baby John. His mom's breathing tube had been removed on the previous day. That was good news but not good enough for her to go home with her baby. The assessment completed on that morning showed that her blood pressure was 156/84, with her temperature a little below 100. She was mildly sedated, her eyes were closed, but her respiratory level had improved again.

Her lab report also showed encouraging signs. It showed that all areas tested revealed excellent spontaneous and cyclic blood flow with good compressibility and a good filling out with augmentation, and that there was no evidence of intraluminal thrombus or other blood clots anymore.

In this condition, she was still not conscious; she was not talking, walking, or even making the kind of movement that would indicate proper recovery. The above conditions caused me to be anxious, having to contend with two special people I loved so much in my life—my wife and the newborn baby, both of whom would not speak to me for many days, weeks, months or years to come. I was tightly held within the grip of a dilemma—the choice between worry and putting my trust in God for strength. I ended this day being thankful to God that my son had been taken home for the first time in 12 days. I was also thankful to my wife's family, who came to my rescue.

DECEMBER 19th
DAY 12
GENERAL PRAYER SESSION ORGANIZED

"Jesus said, 'If you remain in me and my words remain in you, ask whatever you wish and it will be given you.'"

John 15:7

"Praise the Lord O my soul, and forget not all his benefits... who forgives all your sins and heals all your diseases."

Psalm 103:2-3

THE PRAYER SESSION WAS IMPORTANT TO remind us of the tragic situation at hand. Also, the scripture says there are benefits in praising the Lord. In our case, we had placed our supplication before Him for healing and in order to nourish the supplication like a seed planted by the side of a river that bears more fruits, we chose to pray unceasingly.

My wife's improvement continued each day but in different ways. Day 12 was no different. The lungs and chest test report say, "Showed clear anteriority without wheeze with easy respiratory level." Occasionally, she would show purposeful movements, which was an indication that she was likely to follow a command soon. The doctors ordered a minimum level of sedation as they closely watched her neurological status. The report also showed that her blood pressure was up quite a bit, 165/96 with her temperature at 108.

Despite this report, I had noticed that after the doctors' early morning tests and diagnosis, what would occur later in the day tended to be in contrast with their report. I guess because I was always by her bedside, I was more likely to see almost everything and detect changes that a one time daily test could not reveal. An example of this was the significant change I saw in her movement on that day after the doctors had left. I remember commanding her to move her feet, her head and fingers; she did everything I had asked her to do.

During our general prayer session initiated by my father-in-law, he had requested us to specifically offer praises to the Lord. In leading the session he pointed out that a prayerful person must also be a thankful person. It was at this time that I understood the consistency in his message. The first time he mentioned this was when we were at the height of the episode, when my wife had no movement and virtually no sign indicating that she would survive. The message I got then from him through Pastor Bernard Zougouri was that we should stop praying but rather should give praises to God. It was shocking because I just wanted to keep on begging the Lord for her recovery rather than praising Him when I saw no evidence of survival.

To me, the weightiness of a situation determines whether or not it requires supplication or praises. Praises are supposed to be instigated in a cheerful mood. My wife was still terminally ill and I found no reason to praise God. But what I failed to realize was that what seems impossible to man, is possible to God. It was shocking to me also because of my spiritual immaturity. My father-in-law had been at the forefront of trials and tribulations as a preacher in a country that has a high percentage of Muslim population. Perhaps being battle-tested many times, he was in a position to understand what was going on in the spiritual realm better than me. This message and the situation taught me that to follow God you must understand His will.

Giving thanks and praises to God is indeed a necessary aspect of a Christian life in both good and bad times. In I Thessalonians 5:18, the scripture says, *"Give thanks in all circumstances for this is God's will for you in Christ Jesus."* As the session got under way, there was singing, scripture reading and, above all, the giving of thanks. It was a short session that lasted for 30 minutes but leaving that session we all were spirit-filled. Our gathering on that day also demonstrated the fulfillment of scripture. As noted above, in John 15:7, Jesus said, *"If you remain in me, and my words remain in you, ask whatever you wish and it will be given to you."* By gathering in the name of the Lord, and giving thanks and praises, we were watering our seeds of faith in order for them to bear fruit. The day ended well as everyone continued with individual praises.

To sum it up, looking up to God in time of distress, trials and tribulation is a panacea to our problems. When we pray in a joint accord, we experience God's miracle.

DECEMBER 20ᵗʰ
DAY 13
TRANSFERRED TO THIRD LEVEL RECOVERY AREA

"The moon moves slowly, but it crosses the town."

Author unknown

"As for me, I watch in hope for the Lord, I wait for God my Savior; my God will hear me."

Micah 7:7

DAY 13 WAS ANOTHER STEP ON THE SLOW road toward recovery. Nothing had really changed. The blood pressure was up to 160/90. Later during the day it increased to 176/107 when the nurses took a second reading. The doctors added a new medication to the long list my wife was already taking. Her condition regressed a little to the previous status. Actually, the first six hours of this day were dispiriting. My wife had lost the ability to follow commands again, but later during the day she slowly moved her hand to her abdomen around the area of the incision when the nurse asked her to do so. When she moved her hand, the nurse exclaimed, "Surprise cooperation." The nurse later encouraged me to talk a lot to her to keep her awake. She added, "Talking a lot to her will help in her recovery, especially communication."

The slow pace of my wife's recovery was a reminder of the biblical description of life—*"life is like a vapor."* On the morning of December 7th, there were only a few seconds of exchanges: "Daddy, I can't breathe," then, "Okay, I will call the nurses," and, "No, I will be okay." With this, her priceless breath was gone. As one of her nurses put it, "She lost everything on that day."

When she was transferred on this day to the third level, we were told that that would be the last stop because it was a recovery area for all patients. The question about how long they would allow her to stay there depended on her health insurance, so yet another problem emerged. In a few days we would be told to check with the insurance company to verify how long she would be able to stay under insurance coverage. Prior to hearing from the insurance company, the most disturbing news was the initial information they gave us that the third level would be the last stop. The statement was vague from the onset, but when we were told to check with the insurance company, I knew what they meant. With my wife's slow pace of recovery, I wasn't too sure if we could meet their unannounced deadline. Secondly, I didn't know whether or not we would still have the chance to keep seeing a doctor after her discharge.

Worst of all, I feared that if she didn't achieve the required recovery level and the insurance expired, we might be heading for danger.

Worries were necessary and fear was a legitimate concern at this juncture, humanly speaking. I did not have a way to persuade the hospital administration if they were to decide that it was time to go. As I viewed the situation, my wife would still need medical attention for many days to come. The only area within my control was what we had been engaged in—just thanking God for everything. At the close of the day, I was a bit downcast; it was only God that we all looked up to for the next step on the journey. My wife's condition remained on and off for the rest of the day, with no significant improvement in sight.

DECEMBER 21ˢᵗ
DAY 14
ENCOUNTER WITH TRAVELING NURSE ONE

"Why are you downcast, O my soul? Why so disturbed within me? Put your hope in God, for I will yet praise him, my Savior and my God."

Psalm 42:5

"Those who hope in the Lord will renew their strength. They will soar on wings like eagles; they will run and not grow weary, they will walk and not be faint."

Isaiah 40:31

"IT IS NOT UNUSUAL FOR A PATIENT TO leave the doctor's office with many unanswered questions." The impact of day 13 was still upon us as we began a new day. As always, each day has its unique experience. The worst experience of a day comes either in the morning, or in the evening. A lot of the time we were not told the causes of the regression in my wife's recovery. As noted above, a nurse told us, "During recovery from such a terminal illness, you take two steps forward and one step backward or vice versa." Day 14 was one of our worst experiences on the third level.

It was four more days to Christmas and at this time we were convinced that the hospital setting would be our place for celebration, if there were to be any. My father-in-law was still with us. It was definitely a tough time for him as it was for me. He had a lot of commitments back home with his church, but he thought that leaving his daughter in such a condition would be the wrong choice. On this day he phoned his wife, my mother-in-law, to postpone his flight. He told me she was exceedingly glad because she didn't want him to come back leaving their daughter still seriously sick. She wanted him to come back home with the news that she was doing fine. So they all agreed he should stay with us for a while.

From the assessment that morning we understood that my wife was mildly agitated and that her blood pressure was 161/81, and her temperature was at 99.1. Her agitation was on and off; the cause of it had not been determined. At about 11:15 A.M., after another assessment, the nurse suspected that she was in pain but could not find the real cause of her agitation. He administered some pain medications to calm her down. She slept for a while and woke up around noon. Until the next shift, she appeared to be calm and in good condition. She was much more settled as she tried to gaze at anyone who passed by.

At about 9 P.M. everyone who came to visit had gone home. As usual, I took my seat by my wife's bedside, carefully watching for any sign that would prompt me to help. I was already depending on hope and a miracle from God for her recovery and taking into consideration the lost time and the trauma I had been through up to this point, my persistence to see her through was not something I was prepared to compromise. As I sat and watched closely, I noticed my wife tossing and turning on the bed. I asked, "D.Q., D.Q., what happened? Are you hurting?" As expected, she could not say anything since she was still not able to speak. I went on to inspect the bed, thinking she may be lying on some object, but I found nothing. I tried again and again, checking other areas of the bed and still found nothing. The assigned nurse had gone by then, so I stepped out into the corridor, which was about a quarter of a mile long. I couldn't spot anyone, even in the furthest distance. I decided to wait for a while, suspecting that the nurse might have gone to care for other patients. She finally arrived after 15 or 30 minutes. My wife was still rolling on the bed, so I explained what was going on so she could see for herself. She suspected my wife might be in pain, so she went back to her medicine cabinet, brought some medication and administered it. My wife was calm for about 15 minutes, then the pains started up again. The nurse had left, perhaps to check on other patients again. This time I decided to stay with my wife and wait. My wife was very agitated to the point that she became uncontrollable, but I felt I couldn't take a step away from her for fear that she would fall off the bed.

I called the nursing station, but no one was there. Usually, when the nurse leaves, she stays away for about 15 or 25 minutes at most. The farthest I could go was about five to ten feet away and that took me only into the corridor with the hope of finding someone who could help. The nurse finally got back after about 25 minutes. Again, I explained what had been going on. As I was explaining it, my wife was rolling all over the bed in tears before the watchful eyes of the nurse. When I suggested to the nurse that she might still be in pain, she nodded in agreement, left and brought back some more medications and administered them again. The pains kept coming with even greater force each time she administered the pain medications. The night had been far spent; it was about 2 A.M. My wife had been restless throughout this time and no medication she had given her was sufficient enough to stop the continuous pain.

Because of the magnitude of the pain I could no longer hold my peace. I became very angry and demanded an amicable redress to the problem. I became suspicious about the type of painkillers being used that clearly were not helping. At the same time, I was cautious that my insistence to seek proper treatment should be prudent. I had no medical background and did not understand all the specifics. So, I didn't want to push too far in fear of destroying any warmth that had existed between us.

I continued to say things like, "She might be really hurting; if there is anything else you can do, please do it." I guess she didn't respond to my petition because my countenance was different from my tone of voice. Instead, she chose to go on the defensive because I had put her on the spot. All I wanted her to do was to give me an explanation concerning the cause of the continuous pain my wife was experiencing or bring in a co-worker who might have had an idea what was going on. It wasn't so much a question of the immediate suppression of the pain.

Thankfully, it was now about 5:30 A.M. and the next shift would begin at 7 A.M. Usually, the incoming nurse would come in at least thirty minutes early to do some paperwork before the start of the shift. There was nothing I could do further, so I prayed that we might make it to the next shift to find a better solution to my wife's uneasiness. Fortunately for me, the nurse that treated my wife on the previous day was the one that came in next. He was someone you could ask for answers to your questions. I patiently waited for the first nurse to leave. I took the case to the second nurse and explained what had gone on during the night. He told me that it was my right to ask the nurse to see the medication chart. But I said I had not asked her. He took me into the office to show me the chart.

I was surprised by what we discovered. She had not given the medication she claimed to have given. The nurse went on to administer the necessary medication. At this point I wanted to stop fighting; my wife had already been given the right medication and she was asleep. When the nurse told the supervisor, he asked for my opinion and I simply said that I needed another nurse. He agreed and replaced her with another nurse the following night. We ended the night of day 14 on a very rough note. I was told that the night nurse was a traveling nurse.

DECEMBER 22ⁿᵈ
DAY 15
ENCOUNTTER WITH TRAVELING NURSE TWO

"Wait for the Lord; be strong and take heart and wait for the Lord."

Psalm 27:14

"Perseverance must finish its work so that you may be mature and complete, not lacking anything."

James 1:4-5

DAY 15 WAS ANOTHER LESSON IN patience and perseverance. The experience of the previous day was repeated on this day. Because I was prepared for it, I could detect anything that looked like it. I had informed my father-in-law about the incident during the previous night. He decided to stay with me a little longer on this day. My wife had managed the excruciating pains through the night of day 14, surviving till the next day. She appeared restless and frail, to the point that even a spattering of icy cold water could not stimulate her to make an appreciable movement. What she had experienced could better be described as an uncharacteristic incident of wrongful treatment.

Observation by the assessment team on the morning of day 15 found her intermittently agitated, which led to occasional sedation. That in itself, at some level, was a testimony to her experience from the night before. Her blood pressure went up to 194/101, with her temperature at 100. The good news was that her breathing I had been seriously concerned about was clear and even, according to the report.

After the difficult experience on the night of December 14th, I was promised that a different nurse would be assigned to my wife the next night and indeed the promise was fulfilled—a new nurse came and I was hopeful that a better and compassionate treatment would be administered if the irritation recurred. I didn't count it as a victory to have a different nurse due to my action; I thought the hospital had done its best to deal with what I thought was one of many neglectful problems that occur in hospitals every day around the country and elsewhere in the world. But I nervously accepted the apologies and was prepared to move on once a change was made.

As pointed out, based on the experience of the previous night, my father-in-law decided to extend his time with me at the hospital on day 15 before going home at night. At about 9:30 P.M., the pain started again—she tossed, turned, rolled, and even pulled out her feeding tube. I quickly notified the nurse, trying to do everything possible to avoid a replay of the previous night.

Assuming she hadn't been told what had happened, I went on to explain the pain my wife had gone through during the previous night but managed to avoid the details concerning the previous nurse's failure to stop the pain. With this explained, I placed my confidence in her to do what was required within her professional capacity to save my wife from any pain during the night.

Later during the night I realized that the saga of mistreatment would be repeated. After administering the first dose of painkiller, two hours later, at about 11:30 P.M., the level of pain increased again. My wife became even more restless. I intensified the questioning, being that I was confused by what I believed was the inability of those night shift nurses to adequately treat my wife. This time, instead of simply telling the nurse what was happening, it became, "What are you giving this woman that is not helping her?" She told me, "I have given everything she had so far, but I don't know why it is not helping." From what I know about pain, whether it is severe or not, it can be devastating. No matter how one tries to manage it, especially without medication, it is impossible to stop the discomfort.

Research on the subject of pain has found that those who go through excruciating pain can barely sleep at night and become weary the next day, which compounds the problem that leads to more irritability, depression and more pain. They call it a "terrible triad" of suffering, sleeplessness, and sadness, a calamity that is as hard on the family as it is on the victim. That was exactly the problem facing not only my wife, but also my father-in-law and myself, coming out of the previous experience that the nurse didn't seem to understand. Ranting and disorderly behavior were not part of my plan and for that matter are not part of my nature. All I wanted was to get my wife through the crisis by advocating for a better treatment for her, so I kept insisting upon it.

Despite my continuous effort, the problem did not seem to have an end in sight as the night rolled on. My wife got more and more agitated as her dad and I ran from one side of the bed to the other trying to prevent her from pulling out her feeding tube and interfering with other machines that were attached to her bed. My ambiguity about the nurses' provision of services heightened and, not being satisfied by merely repeatedly asking her the same questions over again, I asked to speak with her supervisor. Unfortunately, there was either no supervisor on shift that night or everyone was busy somewhere else in the building. She came back and said there was no one in the office. My intention to see the supervisor was only predicated upon obtaining further help for my wife. He or she might have had another way of dealing with the situation based on experience. The old adage says, "Two heads are better than one." With persistent requests for a second opinion, the nurse left in search of the most senior person she could find to intervene.

Thirty minutes later, she returned with a doctor from the Internal

Medicine unit of the hospital. Remembering the adage, "Two heads are better than one," I was calm when I saw the doctor, believing that the situation would be properly assessed and treated, as it should be. But something else happened when the doctor arrived. After I had explained my side of the story, including all that had happened during the previous night, he asked me the following question: "Did you know that your wife was clinically dead?" The question sent chills through my spine, but I responded quickly, also with the same intensity, "What does that have to do with finding a painkiller?" He went on to say, "The nurses are doing their best to give your wife the treatment she needs." I reminded him that nurses are human beings, prone to being inconsistent and that they sometimes need help, just like anyone else. I cited the example of what I had seen a week before when one of the nurses came in to administer a blood pressure medication to my wife when the reading was 117/72. When I asked the nurse, "Do you give your blood pressure medication regardless of this reading?" the nurse replied, "Oh, I didn't even look at it." I told him, "I am not a medical doctor, but sometimes something requires a common sense approach." He went on to defend the nurse as I also stood my ground to fight back. Thankfully, my father-in-law was around. He kept telling me, "Leave them alone, God knows what He is doing." At the end of my diatribe, the doctor prescribed morphine to be given to my wife for the pain and left.

As I view our discourse, specifically the issue of "clinical death" became a surprising part of the discussion. I found no problem with him telling me the truth about my wife's previous debilitating condition. As part of their profession, I assume doctors don't do so to savor the feeling of telling the truth. What it does is to bring reality to the forefront. On the other hand, without explaining what the outcome would be if you gave pain medications to a patient who was once clinically dead, caused me to doubt his neutrality. Reminding me of the truth was not a solution to reducing the pain; it was only a spur to stir up tension of emotions that were already inflamed.

It was already about three in the morning and the medication the doctor had prescribed helped my wife rest until the end of the shift. We found out again during the morning shift of the following day that some of the pain medications were withheld. I was told that both night nurses were traveling nurses. At this time, I felt enough was enough, so I requested to see the supervisor again to hammer it out once and for all. It was the same supervisor I had met after the first instance. Realizing the seriousness of the matter, he took it beyond his level and called the manager of the department. Before the manager met me, they had already explained the case to her. She apologized and gave me her complementary card and said, "Neither of the two nurses will treat your wife again." On her card there was a direct number to call her if I saw either of the nurses again. Thankfully, that manager helped me get off the

53

emotional rollercoaster I had been on. My wife did not experience any pain again until she was transferred to another department for further recovery.

My experience during those two nights taught me a whole lot. The nights left several indelible questions on my mind. First, if I had not had the chance to be with my wife at the hospital during those nights, what would have become of her for the next week if those nurses were the only ones assigned to her? What would have been the medical report if she had died from such treatment? Perhaps on a much broader level, a debate that continues to occupy our religious and secular teachings today should be raised: What is a timely death? Remembering December 8th, those two nights of excruciating pain also tell me that every patient's relative should be with their loved ones, once admitted to hospital or any healthcare center. Due to those incidences I increased my involvement with my wife at the hospital. I preferred to make myself become a partner in progress, to give the doctors and nurses any help they needed. I thought it would be good for me and good for them as well.

I also thought that between the nurses and patients' family members there should be a symbiotic relationship. Symbiotic to simply mean, helping one another. This kind of relationship, when encouraged, especially by healthcare administrators in every hospital, would help to settle one of the problems we now have in our system today—the disproportionate number of nurses to patients, which I thought was one of the problems that was not unique to that hospital. It is a nationwide concern. Also, by encouraging this, each side would be treated respectfully, as they should be motivated by one purpose—the common good and the survival of the patient. In her book, *"The Politics of Breast Cancer, Waking up and Fighting Back,"* Altman Roberta cites similar frustrations of three breast cancer survivors who said the following: "Doctors are sometimes intimidating unless you really do assert yourself. Sometimes with the doctors you just have to educate yourself."

"I owe my life to the physiatrist. He took me seriously. I was starting to feel like a neurotic woman, all these pains I was having… He said, 'you know, you are not getting better. We have to see what's going on here.'

"The doctors patted me on the head and told me I was being paranoid because my mother had had breast cancer. She felt sure that this was just a fibrocystic disease and that if it would make me feel better I could go have another mammogram. She said I was worrying just because of my mother and not to worry."

The views and frustrations cited here are from real people and real experiences. They are like mine, as you can no doubt appreciate. Most doctors and nurses do not like to be asked because to do so might appear like putting them on the spot, especially if they had planned on administering a specific kind of medication and the patient or a family member tries to find out what it is. Perhaps my many questions to the nurse that night opened a Pandora box of frustration on their part. But again, as a Christian, these challenges come for us to see the strength of the Lord. As my father-in-law rightly said, "God knows what He is doing." The reminder, "Did you know your wife was clinically dead?" perhaps only meant to demonstrate what doctors do when failure is in sight after all measures have been taken. But they usually forget to acknowledge that there is a higher physician who is never in the business of failure and discouragement. He is the physician that treats all illnesses fully with a lasting recovery. He is the only one that has monopoly over the science of healing. He is my wife's physician and mine also. The name of that physician is Jesus Christ, our Lord.

As Altman also noted, "A doctor's medical decisions and demeanor can have a major positive or negative impact on the extent and course of a patient's recovery." There is a lot of truth in this statement. From the onset of my wife's resuscitation at ICU 2600 Level, I realized that the reports I received on a daily basis were mostly discouraging. But God works in ways we won't always understand and He does so to our benefit. I am thankful that my wife did not have the ability to hear all of what we were told at that time. Sensitive as she is, it would have impacted her so greatly that it would have truly impaired her recovery. Now I can say that being non-responsive, motionless, speechless was positive in this regard. But also, these pointers indicate the wonders of God.

The ineffectual behavior of those two nurses on those nights is not typical of that hospital. I had worked there before and knew that there are qualified men and women working there whose sole objective is the patient's wellbeing. The administration is staffed with intelligent people, most of them Christians who look after the hospital activities with keen attention to detail on a daily basis. An example of the management's ability to handle a crisis of such magnitude is the decision taken by the manager who came in that morning to solve the problem I had with the traveling nurses. On the other hand, no human system is ever perfect. No matter how intelligent you are as a manager, there will always be problems with some of the employees. It happens everywhere and at every level.

DECEMBER 23ʳᵈ
DAY 16
ENCOUNTER WITH TRAVELING NURSE THREE

"Encourage one another and build each other up, just as in fact you are doing."

1 Thessalonians 5:11

IT IS SAID, "BEHIND EVERY DARK CLOUD, there is a silver lining." Days 14 and 15 were rough times for us, but we ended them breathtakingly well. There had been incidents of mistreatment for two consecutive nights, but little did we know that another traveling nurse was about to meet us hours later during the night of day 16. The first thing I was usually concerned about in the morning was to know how my wife was doing. One of the ways to know that was through the usual assessment report or by talking to one of the nurses or doctors assigned to her case. According to the team's medical assessment report, I learned that morning that there were slight changes in the rate of my wife's improvement. She was still agitated and her blood pressure was elevated during the morning hours. By noon she became calmer.

I was still not sure who the next nurse would be for the night. The only way to know this would be during the shift changeover. I was somewhat weary, since I didn't want another fight. I entered the evening hours a bit nervous. As we approached the shift changeover time I began to see unfamiliar faces of nurses. I took a deep sigh of relief, thinking one of those faces would be in charge of my wife's care for the night. But that was not sufficient information to settle my nervousness. I had seen unfamiliar faces during the past two nights and that didn't make a difference.

It seemed that the outgoing nurse might have made some form of introduction. When it was about time for the shift changeover in the evening, one of the unfamiliar nurses, with long dark hair, about 5 feet 7 inches, appeared and introduced herself as the one taking over to be with my wife for the night. The staff went through all the procedures for shift changeover and the nurse went back to the nursing station to complete her paperwork. The size of my wife's room was about ten feet by ten feet. My recliner was at the upper right corner of her bed, about three feet away. It was close enough to reach her at any time if there was a problem and she needed help. When the nurse left to complete her paperwork at the nursing station, I took my place on the recliner to pay attention to my wife.

In about 15 minutes another nurse, a bit shorter, and looking calm, came in. All I could observe from the face of this nurse was nothing but beams of smiles. She went around my wife's bed, straightened up her bed sheet and sat on a stool right near her. After about ten minutes she said something I least expected from a nurse after days of fighting with other nurses. She started telling me a story of an experience she had had with a terminally ill woman she once took care of in another hospital. According to her, the doctors had given up on the woman, and many of them believed that the woman didn't have long to live. They said she would die perhaps in a matter of days. As I listened to her telling the story, I began to wonder what she was trying to drive at. *Was she here to tell me that my wife would not survive and if so, why would she come to tell me a story that had no potential to revive me from my aching mind, coming out of days 14 and 15,* I silently wondered.

Being puzzled by her story that seemed not to be ending, I was a moment away from interrupting with a question as to the point of the story when she said, "And then I prayed for the woman." I recoiled into my shell like a snail, instantly swallowing my words and I listened more intently. Just then the main nurse for the night arrived. She too appeared to be friendly as she engaged me with a series of questions and comments about how the night might go. I called it a teaching moment. Now sensing a great friendly and professional atmosphere, again I took a deep sigh of relief that no one else could have noticed, except me. After what appeared to be a brief moment of orientation on how the night might proceed, the nurse went on to see the other patients, assuring me before she left that she would do her best. The other nurse continued her story and in the end she told me, "I am one of the traveling nurses." My countenance changed immediately. Murmuring to myself, I said, "Oh God! A traveling nurse again?"

After she had introduced herself, she sat for a moment and said, "If you don't mind, we can pray." Again I cringed. Now you can imagine how this nurse had been influencing my changing emotions so rapidly every time she said something. The good thing was that all my suspicions quickly vanished and I instantly began trusting the woman like a sister in Christ. Before she left, picking up the rest of the story she had been telling me earlier, she said, "God healed that woman after our prayers." She told me not to worry, my wife would be okay and that by the time she would come back next time, God would perform a miracle for my wife. Apparently, she was also assigned to the same ward, Level 3300, third floor.

It was about 8:30 P.M. when the nurse and I ended our prayers. It was a short prayer session that lasted for about five to ten minutes. Other nurses unintentionally interrupted us when they came in briefly to provide services, but it went well anyway. That night was totally a different kind of night. Things turned around 180 degrees in my wife's favor. She was treated really well and showed no signs of restlessness throughout the night. The nurse was fully engaged with her, making sure that all the required medications were properly administered. At the end of her shift in the morning I was grateful to her and thanked her for her services.

A few days on, my wife's condition changed. The excruciating pain and restlessness gradually vanished. Every evening I made an attempt to find this nurse who prayed with me, but to no avail. I began wondering who this nurse really was. How could she appear so briefly with such encouragement and then was nowhere to be found? Was she an agent of an angel sent to comfort me and pray with me to assure me of my wife's recovery? My speculation ran deep, but it could do nothing to help me find her. What made it shocking was that, before she left me that night, she assured me that she would come back the next day. I assumed that if there were any changes to her plans, she would have come by to see me. I was at the hospital 24/7. Thankfully, the glimmer of hope she left with me materialized into recovery in the end. I believed God was working through many people to build my confidence and she was one of those people.

DECEMBER 24th
DAY 17
END OF FAST AND PRAYER

*"When you pass through the waters, I will be with you; and when you pass
through the rivers; they will not sweep over you. When you walk through the
fire, you will not be burned; the flames will not set you ablaze. For I am the
Lord, your God, the Holy one of Israel, your Savior."*

Isaiah 43:2-3

*"The prayer offered in faith will make the sick person well, the Lord will raise
him up. If he had sinned, he will be forgiven. Confess your sins to each other
and pray for each other so that you may be healed. The prayer of a righteous
man is powerful and effective."*

James 5:15-16

*"We shall continually chant so that we and our children shall never forget that
we are sons of the morning, children of the light."*

Morris Krok

THE DEVASTATION HAD LASTED FOR 16 DAYS, December 9 through
December 24. It was a long and difficult journey. In the long run it paid off.
    Our journey through the waters and fire, and our prayers offered in faith
for the sick by the chanting of the name of the Lord, will remind people that
we are indeed the children of light and our actions by His grace shall produce
victory. When I initiated the one-man fast and prayer and told the Lord I was
going to fast and pray without stopping until my wife was healed, little did I
know that the prayer warriors at my wife's dad's church in Africa were with
me on this bandwagon. Here with us in the United States were also members
of my church who were intensively engaged in prayers. I was convinced that
the confluence of prayers from those many prayer warriors had won the battle.
Again, the healing I sensed on day 17 was not so much due to the solitary fast
and prayer spree I was on; it was also the effort of those who were in the right
frame of mind and worked tirelessly behind the scenes to see this through.
    To this day, I do not know some of those who prayed with me either by
name or by face. Some even prefer not to be known. I say thanks a million
times to all of them for the unwavering love and care shown to my wife, our
baby and myself.
    You may ask, why was a fast needed in the first place? First, I had always

held the belief that an extreme situation requires extreme measures. The incident that took place with my wife was not to be treated lightly; it was extreme in its entirety. It caught me off balance and scattered the plans my wife and I had for our baby and our marriage within a wink of an eye. At that moment when it happened, it drew a huge cloud of uncertainty over me as a Christian regarding my faith in God. In short, I saw it as a test, a test I had never taken before. So, the method I applied in dealing with it says more about the magnitude of the situation and what I hoped the outcome would be. Second, I also chose to fast because the Bible tells me so. When Jesus encountered the devil, He fasted for 40 days (Matthew 4:2); when Moses went up the mountain to receive the tablets of the Covenant, he fasted for 40 days (Deut. 9:9-18); Elijah also fasted for 40 days (1 Kings 19:8). This is just to mention a few of the instances of fast and prayers noted in the Bible. In each of these examples, the situation was grave and required something beyond ordinary prayers.

The third reason why I chose to fast was to seek God's favor in my darkest moment. In Jeremiah 17:10, the scripture says: *"I the Lord search the heart and examine the mind to reward a man according to his conduct, according to what his deeds deserve."* Also, Psalm 18:20 points out that *"The Lord has dealt with me according to the cleanness of my hands He has rewarded me."* As a Christian, seeking God's favor is our primary objective, but to achieve that goal comes with a price. When Jesus said, *"If you want to follow me, take up my cross,"* He spoke metaphorically to mean that it is not all easy sailing, as many of us have deceived ourselves to believe that once baptized, we are forever saved. I wanted the Lord to intervene in my crisis, so for Him to do so, a laid-back approach would only spell out failure, but a genuine effort and a sense of humility at every level of sincerity was required. Again, the Bible tells us in the Book of Matthew, *"He who seeks, finds, he who knocks, it is opened unto him and he who asks, receives."* So, I had to take a leap of faith in such an extreme situation to focus on God as my help in times of trouble.

The judgment call that led me to end my marathon on day 17, after 16 days of fast and prayer, was simply based on what I thought and felt had been secured about my wife's condition. On that day, the nurses spoke to me in the presence of my wife concerning their plans to discharge her. Among the options they gave were the following: to send her to an annex outside of the hospital where she would be able to go through therapy, or to send her home where home health practitioners could see her on a daily basis as she recuperated. She made several attempts to speak, and several attempts to wake up. She did these unusual things that indicated great improvement. While it was true that I had no power of divination to see what the future concerning her recovery would look like, with the strong conviction that the Lord had done His work, I was guided to end my sessions of fast and prayers.

In essence, the scripture noted above, *"The prayer offered in faith will make the sick person well, the Lord will raise him up. If he had sinned, he will be forgiven"* was the foundation upon which I based my conviction that it was time to end my fast. As the day came to a close, I felt that I had learned many lessons from those trials, tribulations and frustrations during the recovery process that progressed and regressed each day. It was inconceivable that we would reach day 17 to finally decide that God had done it. As God would have it, everyone that visited on this day saw exactly what I saw in my wife. She was lively.

From that day onward, her recovery came in rapid successions. She showed great signs of improvement each day in different ways. What was left to contend with after those crucial moments were issues of mobility, and the restoration of her voice. Part of the recovery was being able to move her hands and legs on the bed and opening her eyes.

I was very happy. At about 8:20 P.M. on that day, one of the doctors came round to pay a regular visit. What he said was reassuring. Unlike the other doctors, it appeared he had a different take on the issue, probably because my wife's level of recovery had become more predictable. Looking at her level of improvement, he said, "Therapy would be very helpful in regaining everything else, but it usually takes longer." By then, preparation was already underway to send her to the Rehabilitation Center, an annex to the hospital where most patients are sent for the rest of their recovery period.

At the end of the day, what I realized has a lot to do with the account of Francis MacNutt in his book, "The Prayer That Heals" about praying for healing in the family. MacNutt, an internationally known authority on the healing ministry and author of a groundbreaking bestseller, "Healing" (1974) writes: "What God would like to do and through you is so wonderful that you may find it hard to believe God wants ordinary people like you to bless and heal each other in your families. When you start to pray with others, amazing things will happen to you and to your loved ones. I want to encourage you," he adds, "to believe a truth that Christians today are often too cynical to believe: Jesus will heal his people through your prayers." He summarizes it this way: "Healing does not always come from faith; sometimes it leads to faith." Indeed, the recovery of my wife strengthens my faith.

And so, I learned a lot about fast and prayer throughout this time—first, when we go to God in prayer, our strength is renewed; without prayer, we cannot have fellowship with the Lord because it is by this means that we communicate with Him. Second, it is by prayer that we respond to the word of God, the Bible. Thirdly, we live in times of ambiguity; the only power we have for protection is the power from God. Without a prayerful life we are powerless. There are things that go on in the spiritual realm that we do not understand or cannot see; the only weapon we have against those evil forces is to protect ourselves with prayers. That means that we MUST pray every day. Thessalonians 5:17, teaches that, *"We should pray without ceasing."* I also learned that our prayers should not be seasonal or occasional, but let us do it at all times. I was thankful to the Lord for the strength to go through 16 days of fast and prayers.

DECEMBER 25th
DAY 18
ANOTHER MOMENT OF WORSHIP

"You have made known to me the paths of life; you will fill me with joy in your presence."

Acts 2:28

"If the spirit of him who raised Jesus from the dead is living in you, he who raised Christ from the dead will also give life to your mortal bodies through his Spirit, who lives in you."

Romans 8:11

PRAYER HAD BEEN A CRUCIAL COMPONENT in our approach to my wife's recovery. We were determined to continue as long as it took to see her recovered. Every day that came, as long as she had breath, we took the opportunity to commit her to the hands of the Lord.

That year, 2007, our December 25th Christmas Day was spent at the hospital where we had been fighting to retake what the enemy almost took away—the life of my wife. Unlike the previous years, when friends and family members would gather at our home and my wife would be in the kitchen busy preparing meals, this year was totally a different ball game. She had already spent 18 days in a condition where she still couldn't talk but was making some attempt to do so. The good news was, with no major treatment left to be applied, except for lowering her blood pressure, by taking blood thinner medication, and treating the last portion of the C-section wound, she was well on the way to be discharged, as discussions with doctors and nurses continued.

Christmas, being observed as a Christian holiday, was another perfect time for us to engage in moments of prayer. My father-in-law saw it as another opportunity to gather everyone to conduct a prayer session at the hospital on this day. Gathering on Christmas Day in the United States is a way of having a family reunion. So our assembly on that day could as well be seen to serve a dual purpose—family reunion and thanks giving. The room was a very small place, about ten by ten feet and it could only hold roughly ten people at a time before it was filled to capacity. It was about 1 P.M. when my father-in-law assembled us. The baby was also brought in from the house. My wife was a little sedated but could intermittently open her eyes to look around and then fall back to sleep. My father-in-law had already prepared a short lesson from scripture to be given to each participant. He entitled it "Prayer of Faith."

Because he spoke French fluently with some knowledge of English, he chose to give his exaltation in French, while an interpreter translated it into English. He wrote the script in English and gave me one of the copies to read. He wrote thus: "Lord Jesus, for the complete healing and deliverance of Daniella, let the power of your precious blood flow through her entire body, her soul and her spirit, even if right now, she doesn't feel it. Father, let the Holy Spirit, through this precious blood exercise His power over all spirits of disease, malediction, death and push them away from her life in Jesus Christ's name. Let the Holy Spirit's light, peace and rest envelope her in the name of Jesus, Amen!"

We sang a few songs followed by the exaltation that lasted for about five to ten minutes and he led us in a closing prayer. After the prayer, we tried to make my wife hold her baby—we adjusted the bed so that she would be in a sitting position to be able to hold the baby. She was helpless; she didn't have enough strength to hold the baby. She probably couldn't even recognize her baby and there was not enough consciousness and strength to sit up for a long time, but for a brief moment she held the baby. It was a moment to see; even though she had no strength to hold the baby, it was an emotional time to watch a woman once declared clinically dead and rumored to be dead to be sitting upright with her baby in her arms with partial assistance. This was truly a moment of scriptural fulfillment. The Book of Acts says it all: *"You have made known the paths of life, you will fill me with joy in your presence"* (Acts 2:28). In agreement with the scripture, I believe beyond any doubt that the work of the Lord has made itself known in my wife's life. I was filled with joy beyond description. Later during the day, the baby was taken back home and I stayed on with my father-in-law as we discussed plans related to her transfer to the other facility for physical therapy. He left to go home at 10 P.M. to have some rest before the next day as I prepared my recliner by my wife's bedside, just as I had done each night at the hospital. The day went well; so did the night. She slept well and showed no signs of agitation as before.

My sense of the events of the day was that God was in control. I thought that in a few more days the need for continual intensive care would be over. The fact that my wife was still not vocal was a concern, but realizing how far we had come from complete non-movement and silence to real signs of life, my confidence was growing every day. I knew the Lord was about to complete the miracle He had started.

I also felt that the day gave me a clear idea as to how to be prepared for God's miracle. Many things may be required, but a major one that I thought impacted our situation was as follows: that we should make known our request in prayer to the Lord. My favorite passage in the Book of Matthew (7:7-8: *"Ask and it will be given to you…"*) says it all. This passage demonstrates that if we are in need, we should ask. Our days characterized by intense prayers testified to our desire for help from the Lord.

Secondly, the saying that "Opportunity comes to those who are prepared for it" was real in our attempt to see my wife recovered. The Lord needs to see a sign of our willingness and desire for His help. The Bible rightly teaches that, *"We must fight for our salvation with fear and trembling."* In keeping with this requirement over and over again, we presented to the Lord what we had. First, we recognized that He is the Lord and the only one that could rescue us from the problem. Also, and most importantly, our devotion and commitment were signs of our ardent desire. This day too ended on a good note.

DECEMBER 26
DAY 19
ATTEMPT TO SPEAK

"Everything that was written in the past was written to teach us, so that through endurance and the encouragement of the Scriptures we might have hope."

Romans 15:4

"Those who trust in the Lord are like Mount Zion, which cannot be shaken, but endures forever."

Psalm 125:1

WITH ANOTHER LEVEL OF improvement came another downward trend. December 26th, like other nights of restlessness, showed that the process of healing was not a cut and dried phenomenon. After the good moments we had on Christmas Day, the night of December 26th turned out to be different. Sitting by her bedside that night I saw that my wife didn't get enough sleep. There were a lot of tosses and turns and quite a bit of restlessness from 1:20 A.M. for the rest of the morning hours. The restlessness was minor as compared to the previous nights, but it certainly served as a reminder of what had happened previously. Her blood pressure, which was checked that morning, was fearfully high—163/124 with her temperature at 100. She could not follow commands, as she had been able to on the previous day. She regressed to the former stage and would not cooperate with me or anybody else. Her incision drain was in place and there was only a little opening left to dry up. About twice that night she unintentionally removed the feeding tube from her nose. Replacing it so that she could eat something was very painful to watch. It usually required force to put it in. Whenever it was time to replace it, I would always excuse myself to avoid seeing my wife suffer. I had to step out twice that night while the nurses replaced the tube. By morning, between 6:30 and 10:45 A.M., she had become calmer and more restful as she tried to get some sleep. As it turned out, when she woke up later at about mid-day, she became more active, rapidly moving her hands. Another thing I discovered later during the day was that her upper and lower lips were moving increasingly for a while. I could not make anything out of this unusual movement but I would find out later what that was about.

What we had hoped for earlier continued to happen. She still maintained her body movement—the hands, feet and the turning and tossing were still going on. We were now hoping for the next step to follow—talking or following commands to their full extent, but this did not happen. I must admit, there were frustrations at every level of her recovery. Each improvement level came with a kind of frustration before moving on to another level. At this point, the questions were: *Should I go back to fast and pray for another number of days, to better nail it once and for all? Or, Is my wife's condition ever going to get better from this stage on? Do the doctors understand her condition and do they still want to discharge my wife or send her to a rehabilitation center for further recovery?* As you can tell, there was a sense of retrogression of faith in me again that gave grounds for doubts and faithlessness. It was truly difficult for me to remain consistent in my faith. Every time there was a regression in her recovery, things would change gravely. The on and off journey towards recovery was giving us a sign—a sign that everything was beginning anew. She had to relearn everything all over from scratch. I was far removed from my pessimistic prognosis that the journey was an ongoing one. Plans were already being made by the doctors for physical and speech therapists to be involved. Later during late afternoon, the speech therapist arrived to carry out his first assessment. He was there for about ten minutes and left with a promise to resume a fuller examination the next day. An hour later, the physical therapist also came to conduct his examination. He left after a few minutes to prepare for the next day as well.

At about 7 P.M. the rapid movement of her upper and lower lips was more obvious. You could see that she was making some effort to get some words out, but was trying in vain and then became quiet and later fell asleep, perhaps out of frustration, which I was feeling as well.

As we came to the end of the day, I thought the devil was still at work. But considering what we had been going through, I drew courage from the experience. There was never a day that passed without experiencing some form of difficulties, even in the midst of the signs of recovery. My only choice was to hold on to what appeared to be "mixed blessings." I had had my time of weaknesses; it was now time to maintain strength from the Lord as I continued my prayers with others.

DECEMBER 27
DAY 20
"WHY, WHY, WHY?"

"Be still and know that I am God; I will be exalted among the nations, I will be exalted in the earth."

Psalm 46:10

"Teach me and I will be quiet; show me where I have been wrong."

Job 6:24

AS WE CONTINUED TO FIGHT FOR HER recovery in our daily prayers, it became clear on this day that she was ready to join us in the fight for her life. I assumed the movement of her lips the day before was the beginning of her struggle to speak. You could feel and see her frustration as she attempted again to talk, as her upper and lower lips continued to quiver. She immediately burst into tears when she realized she couldn't get a word out. Her emotional outbreak was reassuring to her dad and myself. We were convinced that she had become fully conscious of what was going on. I was told that if she continued to persevere with what appeared to be an attempt to talk, there would be a possibility that she would be able to soon formulate a word.

Having experienced such a rough sequence of events for 20 days without the ability to speak, the resilience to keep pressing on was already a victory. It was clear that the Lord was about to prove Himself so that those who do not know Him may know that He is God. The Lord said, *"I will be exalted among the nations, I will be exalted in the earth."* What we thought was a period with no end in sight was gradually being eroded away before our very eyes through the grace of God.

Later during the day we would get the first major shock of the recovery period. That shock would give us an idea of how my wife would approach the problem in days to come and what her expectations would be.

I was with her in the room awaiting the assessment team to arrive. The team reported at the usual time for the assessment and later left after they had completed their job. What I saw later in the report showed no major changes, but the blood pressure was 148/88. She was very restful and appeared to show real signs of awareness as she tried to stare at the nurses and everyone who passed by. The movement of her lips that we had observed throughout the previous day was still ongoing but had become much more frequent that morning. She made several attempts to say something, but with a lackluster tone of voice she could not get her message across, which gave rise to more frustration. That continued as she struggled to communicate, but every attempt fell short of her intention to speak.

At about 11 A.M. her dad came to relieve me. I went home to change my clothes and decided to come back earlier since it was boring to be home by myself. On my arrival back at the hospital, they had adjusted her bed in a reclining position and she was sitting with her dad and a few other friends. I was told that in my absence she had made several more attempts again to speak and yet she still could not. Just then, in response to my request, the caseworker in charge of her transition to another annex came in to discuss the situation. We spoke for about ten minutes and ended our discussion with the conclusion that she would be transferred later. From the discussion, it was certain that she would be transferred within a week. The date of the transfer was not specified. When I returned to the room, her dad was still sitting by her bed, this time with three other friends. The room was a bit quiet, but I realized that her dad had been talking with her in their local language. All she did when he spoke was to keenly listen to him and then after a while she would make attempts to talk. She did it again and again, but still could not get a word out. She would also roll on the bed and turn the other way as if she were uncomfortable.

It was now about 8 P.M. and visitors were still coming in while others were leaving. Her frustration increased; you could see it in her facial expression, with intermittent tears rolling down her cheeks. But as it turned out, her fruitless but continuous attempts to voice something would prove positive in the end. Little did we know that God had turned her into a self-made speech therapist. It was a little past 11 P.M. and she was still awake with her dad and myself flanking her on both sides of the bed. Within a blink of an eye, to our amazement she sounded a word. It started by her pulling off her feeding tube and she became quite agitated as she was still trying to talk. She banged on the bed again and again. We both started talking to her to calm her down. The biggest shock of the night that helped to end the day on a happy note had arrived. As she persisted to try to talk, weeping and banging on the bed, pulling off everything that was attached to her—the feeding tube, IV, etc., suddenly we heard: "Why? Why? Why?" and she again burst into tears. She kept on asking, "Why, why, why?" which was the only word that she managed to pronounce. Thanks foremost to the glory of God as well as her persistence, she succeeded in the end. That was typical of my wife—persistency.

Her sister once told me that whenever my wife wanted something done, she would struggle at all costs to get it done. In the five years of our marriage she confirmed this to be true by her actions; even when we submitted our supplications to God, she would always work at it in her prayers and act practically toward it until we succeeded. Her asking why, why, why, as the only word we could possibly understand was a huge stride in the persistency she was known for. It also gave us more confidence to end the day. Asking why, why, why at about 12 midnight was a winning goal—we couldn't ask for more; the day for us was a complete breakthrough. Those leaving to go home would now have something to tell the others who weren't there to see the miracle.

The expression, why, why, why—a word she had not mentioned throughout the 20 days, and especially the way she said it through her tears—was enough for us to sense her level of frustration. Looking at the scriptures, one could agree that the use of the word *why* is not unique to my wife; it is a common question among believers and Christians. We had learned about it from similar experiences described in the Bible. For example, when Job's faith was tested by the devil and he realized that his situation had become a heavy load to carry, he asked: *"Why did I not die in the womb? Why did I not give up the ghost when I came out of the belly? Why did the knees prevent me? Why the breasts that I should suck?"* (Job 3:11-12). Job's frustration could be understood from a number of perspectives. First, he was a man after God's heart; he tried hard to live for God in the best way possible. To live for God in the way he did and to be treated by the devil so mercilessly was not only frustrating, but disappointing as well. Second, as a man he tried to withstand the carnage the devil brought upon him and his family, but there was little he could do. So, being close to giving up as a human, Job had no other alternative but to ask, "Why, why, why?" Also, in Mark 15:34, we learned of Jesus' encounter with the Roman soldiers. When he was nailed to the Cross at Calvary, He cried out, *"My God, my God, why hast thou forsaken me?"* Speaking as a man, born of the spirit and of the flesh, Jesus' frustration with man deepened at that moment. But being the Savior, He said, *"Father, let your will be done."*

My wife's faith is incomparable to that of Jesus' or even Job's and what I can say is that since I have known her, she has demonstrated what it means to have a contrite spirit. To have a contrite spirit means to be repentant, to have a broken spirit, to be humble, to be remorseful and to be penitent. To be able to say I am sorry to your fellow man and to God for the wrong you have done takes heart. I cannot say how many times my wife has said sorry to me or to others in order to make things right before sunset. Even if she was driving and wasn't sure when she was coming home, she would call to ask for pardon after an argument before it was too late. The importance of being contrite as a Christian is that it shows our human side. We are not perfect and the only way we can better serve God is when we come clean and confess that we were wrong. Among Christians today, we put up a lot of defense mechanisms, to the extent that those on the other side of the aisle don't seem to know our real truth.

It is a generally accepted truth that regardless of our religious affiliation or social status as human beings we are extremely intricate creatures. We can be found to be deceptive, dodgy, shrewd and unfaithful. It takes a mind reader to understand our inner thought processes in order to know the level of our sincerity when dealing with one another. More often, when we are challenged with the truth, we put on our armor of self-defense, drawing facts and conclusions mostly from areas unrelated to the matter at hand to the detriment of those we are hurting. We ignore a simple word of regret, to say, "I am sorry" which is the basis and the beginning of our journey with God. Most often, we tend to forget that. In other words, we must have the spirit of repentance or a contrite spirit to be able to receive the Lord. My wife is not perfect; like everyone else, she strives for perfection, to live by putting God first in almost everything she does. Following such attempts to live for God in this world of uncertainty, to then see yourself fall into the grips of the devil and realize you do not even have a voice to speak out to tell God your problems, the question "Why, why, why?" would be relevant and understandable to anyone who could hear it.

As I see it, while many of us may engage with the "why" question, it is always the will of God that must prevail. He makes no mistakes. In all of the examples cited above, including my wife's, He has made the point to prove to man that He is God and will always be exalted among the nations and on the earth. As you will learn later, the doctors and nurses also glorified His name.

That day was the first time since my father-in-law had arrived from Africa that he was able to smile; I saw that as a great relief. We all were so thankful to the Lord, more than ever before.

DECEMBER 28th
DAY 21
RESPONDING TO VERBAL PROMPTS

"Therefore my heart is glad and my tongue rejoices; my body also will live in hope, because you will not abandon me to the grave, nor will you let your Holy one see decay. You have made known to me the paths of life; you will fill me with joy in your presence."

Acts 2:26-28

"If the spirit of Him who raised Jesus from the dead is living in you, He who raised Christ from the dead will also give life to your mortal bodies through his spirit, who lives in you."

Romans 8:11

IT WAS INTERESTING TO SEE THE REPORT from the generalized assessment that was provided that morning, after another day that had ended on a happy note. Her lungs were clear, eyes open wide, fully awake; she followed directions accurately and responded to verbal prompts and painful stimuli. However, the upper number of the blood pressure was a little high, 148/80 and the temperature was also higher than normal. Apart from the blood pressure and the temperature, everything else was good. Despite this good news we were mindful of the old phenomenon—two steps forward, one step backward—and hoped that this would not be the case this time. To come back from a condition where everything was gone (speech, body movement, neuro-activities and sight), we were thankful to God for her ability to gradually regain her lost skills.

To confess, the journey so far, as indicated, had not been trouble-free, as you may have noticed. For me, I have viewed it through many lenses, based on doctors', nurses' and other people's perspectives. I have tried to stay calm on the outside, but my innermost thoughts were a battleground each day up to this point on Day 21. When I was alone with my wife at night I would take on the role of a therapist: physical therapy, speech therapy etc. Each night, every moment of solitude I had when the nurses were gone to see other patients, I would begin my routine. I would talk as much as I could to make sure that even if she didn't speak, she would have heard me talk. Physically, I would move her hands or open her eyes while at the same time telling her to look at me. I did all of this to dispel the negative voices I kept hearing that, "It is all over, your wife will not survive…" I wanted to be surprised to see her time of silence turned into the sound of speech. I never ceased working with her, even though she didn't participate in my therapy, but I felt that it was necessary to make those attempts.

On this day, realizing that she was responsive to verbal prompts and having heard her asking, "Why, why, why?" on the previous day, I knew a perfect time had come for me to try something new. The opportunity to do so would usually occur at a time when there were either few people around or I was by myself with her. It was about 3:30 P.M. and several community friends had come to visit. The condition she was in was quite comfortable. She was calm and quiet. They all seemed to be pleased about her condition. Each person expressed happiness, encouraged her and wished her a speedy recovery. Later, almost every one of them left except for one friend—Younger—who was always the last to leave, making sure that it was time for my wife to sleep and that there was nothing else she could help with for the day.

She stayed with us after the others had left. Now, at about 6 P.M., I realized that it was time to begin some therapy to get my wife to do something new before the end of the day. Because of the body movements that she had demonstrated that day, I thought there was more we could do, as we moved into the evening hours. We talked to her several times, but we could not get her to say anything new. However, we assumed she was listening to us and could hear us, except that she was still not too responsive.

With the failure of this attempt, another idea came to my mind. I took a piece of paper and a pen to let her write something down. In order to give her an idea of what to do, I wrote the following lines (see details of our communication below):

E T S U

(A)

(B) Daniel

Karambiri

73

The writing you see is the original script of our communication. The written words are mine and those that appear to be in italics are hers.

I actually wanted her to write the same words that I had written but, as you can see, her writing produced a lot of frustration. The writing didn't make sense, so my emotional state escalated and I began to worry. Younger, our friend was still with me at the time. She looked at me and I looked at her; I noticed she was fighting back her tears, trying hard not to succumb to negativity, having seen those writings. My vision of recovery became even more distant from what I had initially hoped for.

As far as that day was concerned, I regretted that I wasn't content with the major improvements we had made, as described in the morning report: "Calm, quiet, responsive to verbal prompts and being visually alert." But as the scripture puts it, there was still reason to believe that God would not abandon my wife to the grave nor would He let her further decline. I also firmly believed that the spirit of Him who raised Jesus from the dead was living inside my wife and that He would also give life to her. God never does anything in halves. Every work He has done that I know of has always been complete, and I believe He didn't target my wife to be the exception. Healing her was no longer within the power of the doctors; they had predicted long ago that it was going to take His miracle to heal her. So the idea of thinking which medication was needed to take her further on this path of recovery never occurred to me. Confronted with this last frustrating piece of news, we held on until the end of the day.

DECEMBER 29th
DAY 22
FEEDING TUBE REMOVED TEMPORARILY

"Jesus said, 'Which of you, if his son asks for bread, will give him a stone? Or if he asks for fish, will give him a snake? If you then, though you are evil, know how to give good gifts to your children, how much more will your father in heaven give good gifts to those who ask him?'"

Matthew 7: 9-11

"God will yet fill your mouth with laughter and your lips with shouts of joy."

Job 8:21

WITH TWO DAYS TO GO IN 2007, I WAS STIILL in a searching and questioning mood. I wasn't tired of communicating with the Lord about what I needed, which was the total recovery of my wife. Almost the entire month of December had been a nightmare. Looking back, I can see my newborn baby as the only great blessing of the year, as we had been struggling for the survival of his mother who barely clung to life in that realm between life and death.

The Lord instructs, *"Ask and it shall be given; seek and ye shall find; knock and it shall be opened."* What I had asked for, sought after, and petitioned for, had kept me lingering cautiously to receive from the Lord. It was for the exact condition my wife was in before her admission for delivery. Being reminded of the passage *"The Lord will never give you what you didn't ask for,"* I was confident and hopeful, as the previous day came to an end, that the Lord was still in control. The situation was also reminiscent of the words of Job that *"God will yet fill your mouth with laughter and your lips with shouts of joy."*

I also believe that patience is an important lesson here. God had given us all of these promises and assurances, but if patience and faith were neglected, the road to recovery would not only be an uphill journey but would also be quite antagonizing. At this juncture, it was God's time that mattered most to me as far as my wife's recovery was concerned.

By December 29th we had been through 22 days of intensive medical resuscitation; there were fasts and prayers within and outside of the hospital walls and across continents; most people, including some doctors, now believed that as it had not occurred during the first few days, it was now becoming impossible for death to be the outcome. What still remained certain to the minds of other people was that full recovery was not possible. They believed that the chances of being impaired were high. So with one group believing in one thing and another in something different, to predict the outcome one would have to have been inspired by the prophetic ability of Elijah or Isaiah. Faithfulness can best be seen at difficult times. That is when the faith of Christians can bear fruits.

It was about 9 A.M. that day; the blood pressure had gone up again to 151/94 and my wife's temperature was at 102. There was no other regression in her health status apart from the blood pressure and the temperature. She had been on Coumadin to thin her blood to ensure there would be no more clots. That morning the doctor ordered the dosage reduced, which suggested that there was further improvement. What we also learned that morning was that her continuous pulling off of the feeding tube was no longer considered a mistake or non-purposeful behavior as the nurses had made us previously believe. With her level of awareness, and asking, "Why, why, why?"(as we had witnessed during the previous day), we assumed that she wanted the tube taken away from her nose. During the early morning hours of day 22, she pulled it out several times. Because reinstalling it was painful, as one could tell from the anguish she expressed facially when it was being done, I decided that they should hold off from re-inserting it for a while, until it was time to feed her. Consequently she had about six or more hours without the tube in her nose. She was restful and turned and tossed freely on her bed. In order to give her a better day of relief, we also reclined her bed, as it had now become a routine. We did that, so that she could sit up and rest her back properly.

That temporary removal of the tube served as a reminder that the Lord will not give His children a stone when they ask for bread. The full recovery of Daniella, my wife, was what I had asked for, not for a Daniella with drips, feeding tubes and IV lines hanging off of her. My level of confidence increased again and I believed that the best days were yet to come. That day almost everyone that came to visit had one question to ask, as if they had rehearsed it: Is she eating now without the tubes? They were amazed, just as I was. My facial expression with beaming smiles provided the unspoken answer to their questions.

My wife is a good-humored person. She always loves to make people laugh. That day, she was so peaceful. She smiled radiantly at everyone. For about two to three hours they wouldn't stop the jokes. In the end some would say, "You scared us a lot, what were you doing to us?" as if she had done it intentionally.

The jokes, as I view them, were necessary. Her friends made her laugh. Laughter in itself is a healing balm and I thought it was much needed. This therapy, even though she didn't talk back, was enough to give her more awareness. She was peaceful, calm, quiet and kept the dimples of laughter on for a while.

Going back to God in prayer at the end of the day, I asked the question: *"Lord, would you allow my wife to come this far into her recovery without completing what you began?"* And then I would remind myself of His promises, again saying, *"As a good father, who knows how to give good gifts, I trust, believe and know that what happened today is a sign of the many good days ahead."* As you can see, my action may have appeared habitual, but that was only to help describe the attitude of a desperate man in search of an answer. Even at this point I continued to view the situation like a race that is never won until the finish line becomes the decider. So, like any loving husband, wife, son, daughter etc. should, I was only doing what I had to so that the Lord would finish His job.

DECEMBER 30th
DAY 23
"I WANT SOMETHING TO EAT!"

"O Lord my God, I cried unto thee and thou hast healed me."

Psalm 30:2

DECEMBER 30th WAS EXACTLY 23 DAYS SINCE the fateful day of the blood clots that tore my family asunder. But like a flood, the intensity of the terminal illness developed from the clots, receded immensely on this day.

The day started like any other normal day. My wife was calm, quiet, with her eyes open. She stared at the walls of the room and so purposefully at the nurses who came to treat her, as though she wanted to say something. In terms of talking, the only thing we had heard so far was the "Why, why, why?" she had uttered a few days before. I was hoping that only God's miracle could take us through another stage. So, even though she appeared so calm and stared intently at people and objects, it never crossed anyone's mind that she was ready to make a significant move. Beginning that day all I had in mind was to keep the hope alive.

Later, I would learn that her intense look at people and objects was predicated upon real development. The healing hands of the Lord would be revealed and another miracle was about to take place that would send shock waves of surprise through the walls of the Level 3300. It was about 10:15 A.M. and I had just helped the nurses change her clothing, get her dressed and make up her bed. Her feeding tube had not been put back in yet. They were about to connect it to feed her and then remove it when she was done. A few minutes later, while I was sitting on the recliner waiting for the nurses to reconnect the feeding tube, she turned onto her back and looked up at the ceiling. Because she was so quiet, I decided to come closer to her to see if she needed something.

As I stood over my wife, something happened that reminded me of this scripture: *"Because of the Lord's great love, we are not consumed, for His compassions never fail. They are new every morning, great is your faithfulness"* (Lamentation 3:22-23). The Lord was about to fulfill one of His promises that morning in a compassionate and loving way. As I was standing over her, she turned towards me and said, "I want something to eat." Her voice was shaky as she tried to talk. As I stood there looking at my wife, and hearing her say those words, it was like a dream. It took me almost 40 seconds to realize that the voice I heard was truly my wife's voice. The shakiness didn't matter to me; I went running out of the room to get the nurses to quickly get her something to eat. This was the first time in 23 days that I could clearly hear a full sentence from my wife.

That moment, as I look back, was one of the greatest moments I have ever had with my wife—hearing her making that request. It was a moment I had long waited for but didn't know or wasn't too sure when it would arrive. It was unimaginable. For seconds, I stood spellbound and mute. *Was it the Lord revealing Himself to me?* I wondered as I gazed at her quietly. But as I remembered my old Bible stories, pondering over what had just taken place, I realized that this incident could not be very different from Jesus' encounter with the Samaritan woman at the well. The excitement and surprise it created in the woman, as Jesus revealed Himself to her, made all the difference.

The scripture says, *"And after Jesus had told her about her past, she left her water jar and went to town to tell the people about a man who told her everything that she had done…"* (John 4:7-27). As I stood over my wife that day, hearing her say, "I want something to eat," for the first time in 23 days—that moment was revealing. I imagined myself in the shoes of the Samaritan woman who wasn't expecting Jesus at the well, a woman who had never thought of her salvation until that moment came to pass. One could argue that Jesus had no reason being there and had no reason for doing what He did. The Samaritans and the Jews were not friends. He appeared to her because it was time to heal this woman of her sins. He also revealed the woman's past life to her so that she would believe He was the Lord. That miracle that made the woman run into town to tell the people what she had seen was the same miracle that stunned me that morning and caused me to run around Level 3300 searching for the nurses to come and feed my wife because she had requested something to eat. My faith in the Lord was reaffirmed once more. Many of us today think, "Seeing is believing," because of this, others believe that there is no God. Even though the mountains, the rivers, oceans, valleys are testimonies to His existence, they need some godly figure to stand before them and say, "I am the Lord, you've been doubting." For me that morning it was more than His appearance. I had believed in His existence before in many ways; this day my belief was strengthened like the Samaritan woman's.

That moment, if anyone were to ask me, "When would you like to go to heaven?" without hesitation, my answer would be, "NOW!" Now, because I felt cleansed by the miracle. When I was told in the beginning that my wife was clinically dead, and rumors had it that she was actually dead, and later others said she was brain dead and that even if she survived she would be totally dependent on me, little did I know that I would see this level of improvement on this day.

With the progression of my wife's recovery and the ardent prayers of others, I had gained complete confidence at this time, believing that there was no more turning back. On the question of love, to me it was not in question;

after all, love was the one thing that had kept me by my wife's bedside for the previous 23 days of intensive care to help see her through. Worries vanished through my sense of confidence, based on her daily progress. I could also see and feel the same sense of confidence in almost all of the nurses, doctors and administrators who had been following my wife's progress ever since she was coded on day one. In order to refresh my newfound spirit of confidence, I had to employ my sense of humor to make myself and others feel the fresh air of change. I entertained visitors and nurses with light jokes. Humor had actually been my passion. I wouldn't like to do it professionally, but at any given chance, at my leisure, I would never resist my desire to entertain folks with some laughter. But when the evil struck on that fateful day, all the tools and mannerisms to make people laugh were taken away from me. As the daily progress report began producing a sense of normalcy, and from what I was observing each day, I was happy that the good old jokes would soon return.

The request my wife made to have something to eat was a welcome demand both to the doctors and myself, but based on their professional assessment, they felt it would be premature to have her eat anything solid. They preferred to conduct a swallowing test first in a couple of days or so, before allowing her to eat anything solid. So, to begin with, they recommended things like ice chips and anything in liquid form. Under this condition she had no choice but to be patient and wait for the appropriate time before she would have the chance to eat any solid food. The doctors' postponement created a lot of problems for us. On that day alone, my wife made several requests for food.

Being hungry and wanting something to eat was good news. I was exceedingly glad about this but more specifically, I was delighted by the fact that because my wife could now speak simple sentences to communicate her desires, a lot of speculations we had had in the past were no longer valid. So throughout that day, I was in and out of the nurses' station, bringing ice chips to make my wife eat as much as she could. She fed on ice chips and some puddings for the rest of the day.

Some people consider these miracles that take place each day as normal occurrences. They credit them in some cases to the work of science. As I have noted, the survival of my wife is partly due to the medical intervention, but as I have also argued, and has been confirmed by the doctors, there is a limitation to the work they do. I believe that when the doctors' efforts are limited, the rest becomes the work of God.

In the case of my wife, many of the doctors confirmed later that her survival was beyond their work. Who then would it be? As an educated person, I am not in the business of drawing comparisons between science and God, simply because in my Christian life I have chosen not to use the Bible to define science or use science to dishonor the work of God. But understanding what our limitations are as humans, it is fair to say there is a supernatural being above us whose works are far beyond our understanding. I derived the title of this book based on the happenings on day 23, because I believe God's miracle was at work.

I believe that being so confident in the healing power of time on this day was made possible by the power of God. I could not have done it by myself. So the question how well I remember all of the dwindling moments that scared me, frustrated me, kept my faith at distance and left me with nothing but an empty being, is all left to history. My firm belief is that 23 days will go down in my family history as a period of miracles, misery, faith, the surge of medical disorders and tragedies—all of which I experienced during this time. *The scripture says, "Now all has been heard; here is the conclusion of the matter: fear God and keep his commandments, for this is the whole duty of man"* (Ecclesiastes 12:13).

CHAPTER 4
PHASE TWO OF RECOVERY

DECEMBER 31ˢᵗ, 2007
THERAPEUTIC TREATMENT

"For if, when we were enemies, we were reconciled to God by the death of His son, much more, being reconciled, we shall be saved by His life."

Romans 5:10

ECEMBER 31ST BEGAN ANOTHER PHASE of our stay at the hospital. After many relentless days of hard work on the part of the nurses and doctors to do what was in their reach, we were told that the journey had not ended but would continue with what is known as therapeutic treatment. When we think of the word therapeutic, it is a word commonly used within the medical community to suggest another kind of treatment without necessarily the application of medications. As an adjective it means, "healing, restorative, curative, remedial, salutary or beneficial." Generally in the medical context, "it is a system of treatment adopted to correct clinical pathological situations." Therapy is designed to cure diseases. More specifically, it points to the kind of "aggressive intervention programs that come in many forms but generally adhere to behaviorisms, social learning, or cognitive behavior models that are designed to reinforce pro-social behavior."

The doctors had told me that my wife needed many kinds of therapy: walking, speaking and eating, to mention a few. The implication here is that in the course of the blood clots, and subsequent clinical death, she had lost almost everything. So, those programs designed to reinforce her pro-social behavior were highly recommended on a daily basis. The time span for such treatment was not known but a lot would depend on two things: the pace of recovery and her insurance, as we were being advised to check with her insurance agency.

As we prepared for therapeutic treatment, which was planned to take place at Northside hospital, the doctors made some recommendations that she would have to adhere to when eventually discharged from the rehabilitation center to finally go home. One of those was home health services—a continuation of therapy.

On this day she was scheduled to go for a swallowing evaluation at 10 A.M. This was in response to my request; given the continuous pressure I was receiving from her on a daily basis, complaining of hunger to eat something. It was my hope and prayer that when the evaluation was over, there would be a positive result that would enable her to eat solid food. Being able to eat solid food would be another positive step forward in her recovery. She had had a night of complaints, not only wanting to eat but also wanting to get down from the bed. She rolled to every corner of her tiny bed trying to get up throughout the night. But with the wound VAC (vacuum assisted closure) still attached to her abdomen, I could not help her sit up. I called the nurse to let her know what I was encountering. She also felt it was not safe to let her stand, even though she had been bedridden for a long time. The only option I had left was to let her know that for now we couldn't help her to stand up for her own safety. The doctors maintained that the peripherally inserted central catheter (PICC) line be maintained until she would finally pass the swallowing evaluation. She was able to tolerate the procedure successfully. It was placed into the right arm. For me, it was always difficult to watch my wife being pierced with a needle during the installation of the PICC.

The evaluation would be the second attempt; there had been a preliminary test conducted several days before. The result was that she had no problem chewing, but she did have problems swallowing. Because of that, they had to reschedule another examination to make sure that there was no problem swallowing for fear of aspiration. They advised me to continue feeding her with ice chips and similar kinds of food. It was a frustrating piece of advice but necessary in order to avoid problems. They preferred to keep the tube in until the evaluation was completed. When I later asked about the time of the evaluation, a nurse told me that it would be done in a couple of days. Again, they wanted a few more days of monitoring for more improvement.

A few hours after my conversation with the nurse about the postponement of the evaluation, I learned something else. This time, it was about my wife's insurance. They told me that the insurance was about to expire. With this information, our days at the hospital appeared to be numbered. Yet her schedule for the test was still not known. All we had to do was to wait and see how they would deal with the problem. We were also looking forward to information concerning the rehabilitation center schedule. That too was not ready. Our expectations regarding timings for the evaluation and transfer to the rehab center began fading away, partly due to our frustration and worries concerning the expiration of her insurance. The next day would be New Year's

Day, January 1st, 2008. Usually we observe the 31st by making resolutions, asking God for changes in our lives in the New Year, as we make our plans. On this day it would be different. Apart from this tradition, there was something else I remembered on this day. It was exactly the 31st of December 2006 when my mother-in-law called, to give us a prophecy about a child that her daughter would have in the year 2007.

As God would have it, her prophecy was validated with the birth of our son, Baby John. On the other hand, the person with whom I was supposed to be celebrating the fruitfulness of this prophecy was still lying in a little cubicle at the hospital, struggling for survival, and didn't even know whether or not she was a mother. So, two things would be missed on this day. The first would be a resolution—we would not be making a joint family resolution that year. If there were to be any resolutions, they would have to be made by me alone to reflect all I had petitioned for during my fast and in prayers—God's healing of my wife. Second, there would be no reflection on the previous December 31st as a day that made its way into our family archives, due to the prophecy of my in-law. But there was also another thing we would be missing. Apart from resolution making, and a time of reflection about what my in-law had predicted, the fun time associated with New Year's celebrations would also be missed. The nice food, several visitations, gifts sharing…

This meant that Christmas and New Year's Day's celebrations fell off the radar screen of our family gathering for the year 2007 and early 2008. I thought to myself that this was one way to measure the loss of something or someone important. That day I realized that most nurses had perhaps gone home to visit with friends or family to have fun. It was a day that usually sends people off the streets, away from work or some other busy schedules to be at home. Fewer nurses were on shift that day.

My father-in-law and other relatives of my wife were still at the hospital. It had been roughly two weeks since the arrival of my father-in-law. The longest he had spent during his visits with us before had been only four days. But given the magnitude of his daughter's illness, not only did he choose to postpone his trip back home but he also chose to cancel most of his meetings, conferences and other travel plans. And so, by December 31st he had still not planned on leaving and wasn't sure when he would be going. All we could do on this day was what we had done before: pray, pray and pray. Our New Year's Day celebration took the same pattern as on Christmas Day. My wife's cousins brought the baby to the hospital and once again, we all surrounded my wife, in her tiny bedroom, sang a few songs, read from scriptures, gave praises and prayed until the end of the 31st of December.

JANUARY 1st, 2008

"Wherefore comfort yourselves together, and edify one another, even as also ye do I."

1 Thessalonians 5:11

JANUARY 1ST WAS DAY TWO IN PREPARATION for therapy at the rehabilitation center. Improvement in my wife's condition had become obvious as it continued every day with new signs. She made several more attempts to talk and interacted with our visitors but her voice was still too unclear, even though her messages were understood. Her speech was slurred, but she would manage to get some words out to express her thought.

With no specific time schedule yet for the transfer, and with January 1st being a holiday, there was no need to bother any of the nurses on that day regarding any plans. It was a day we too needed for reflection and to discuss plans regarding our unknown new location. The day was virtually a free day in some sense since there were fewer staff members on shift to carry out the day's activities. Also, because prayer was high on our agenda each day, we prayed without ceasing. January 1st was the perfect day to have more time by ourselves in prayers, without many interruptions by nurses.

All the nurses had to do was to give medications, do some assessments if needed as a routine and leave until the next time when the medications were due. The nurses from the OBGYN had a slightly different assignment. They had previously installed the wound VAC to suck out the superfluous fluid and blood in order to facilitate the healing of the incision from the C-section. Because of this, they made regular routine visits, sometimes twice a day, or came if there was an emergency with the machine. The most important thing, apart from the routine treatment by the OBGYN nurses, was the effort they made to remove the incision VAC before my wife was due to be transferred for therapeutic treatment. We were initially told that the healing of the incision would take up to a few days. At 10:35 A.M. on this day, the nurse came in to check on her. After her inspection, she recommended that we keep the VAC on for a few more days. Since the incision was not a major problem, the change of schedule in removing the VAC didn't worry us much. The day ended with no stress or agitation, but rather quietly, with some family members and friends and church members.

JANUARY 2ⁿᵈ, 2008

"I beseech you therefore, brethren, by the mercies of God, that ye present your bodies a living sacrifice, holy acceptable unto God, which is your reasonable service. And be not conformed to this world; but be ye transformed by the renewing of your mind, that ye may prove what is that good, and, acceptable, and perfect will of God."

Romans 12:1-2

AT 7 A.M. JANUARY 2ND, THE USUAL activities were already underway, including shift changeover, medication administration, the assessment of patients, other kinds of tests performed and a whole host of other activities. As for our family, the rotation of schedule, as arranged, also took place at this time of day, mostly between 9 and 10 A.M. At about 10 A.M. that morning my father-in-law came in to relieve me. I went home to change my clothes and attend to other things.

On my return, the report from the assessment done in my absence that morning was in. My father-in-law was there when they conducted the assessment. It says the following:

"The patient is unable to show two fingers to command; she has tendency to lose focus on task. She appears to be moving all four extremities. Minimum movements are noted in the lower extremities. Activities of living/mobility dysfunction secondary to anoxic encephalopathy, with extensive hospitalization. The patient would benefit from continued physical, occupational and speech and language therapies. The patient would not be able to tolerate a three-hour program at present. This may well be something to work on in the future. I would suggest considering processing with providing services at a sub-acute level, such as available at a skilled nursing facility. The patient had been examined and interviewed, and the chart reviewed. I have discussed the situation with the father. I will discuss with the nurse liaison. Pre-certification needs for Blue Care will need to be explored."

It was pretty clear from this report that we would have to work on two things. First, it appears that a transfer was not planned for any time soon. The conditions for therapy were not yet met, especially since, according to the doctor's remarks, my wife was not fully responsive in terms of following commands as given. Second, now that the issue of my wife's health insurance with Blue Cross had been brought up in print, we would also have to deal with that head-on if we wanted to go for therapy. Concerning not being fully responsive, I have always had some qualms regarding the medical team's assessment report. For example, prior to the main assessment that morning before I left, a nurse came in to administer the 8 A.M. medications. Sensing how agitated my wife was, rolling on the bed, the nurse decided to calm her down calling her by name, "Daniella," trying to get her attention. My wife turned her head to look at the nurse. The nurse sat with her on the bed and said, "I love you." She replied and said, "I love you too." The nurse noted, "She was much more responsive and looked much better today."

In my mind, her failure to respond to the doctor's command could be based on her sheer refusal or because she was not in a good mood and did not wish to interact with anyone. We were waiting for the swallowing evaluation schedule when this report came in. Given the gravity of it and based on the doctor's skepticism, we could not insist on the evaluation, as we would have preferred. With what seemed to be few more days left to the transfer, we didn't want to derail the process. But we were convinced that her ability to chew the ice and her continuous requests to eat were satisfactory indicators that if she were to be taken for a swallowing evaluation again, she would do well.

Having read the report, I found the general context to be disheartening. For example, expressions like "extensive hospitalization based on anoxic encephalopathy; patient would benefit from continued physical, occupational and speech and language therapies," all appeared to indicate that the recovery process was nowhere in sight. On the other hand, these expressions by now had become norm to me; as humans we tend to be somewhat shaken whenever doctors say uncomfortable things to us. But within us we knew that God was about to complete His miracle.

JANUARY 3rd, 2008
"I WANT TO HAVE A SHOWER"

"It is the sovereign Lord who helps me. Who is he that will condemn me? They will all wear out like a garment; the moths will eat them up."

Isaiah 50:9

LONG AGO I HAD A CONVERSATION WITH a friend. He had just been through some difficult moments in his life that involved a lawsuit. According to him, someone had falsely accused him of something he hadn't done. The case was so difficult for him that he wondered every day how he was going to get out of it. Cases that involve litigation are long, drawn-out procedures. But according to him, his second appearance in court settled the matter and the opponent was charged with perjury.

The manner in which the case turned around made him see the work of God from a much broader perspective. He describes it this way: "Nowadays, God is in His athletic suit going around redeeming His children from trouble." Confused by this, I asked, what does that mean? He said, "Athletes, for example soccer players, are ubiquitous on the field of play. They are always on the run when the ball is in play, running after it everywhere on the field to score a goal. Placing God in an athletic suit, I am only trying to describe how He was right there in the courtroom with me."

He continued, "Many people, including myself, believe that everything with God requires patience, but I think it is not true in many cases, as I have come to realize in my recent experience. With my legal problems recently, the way I got out of them so quickly—I believe it was only God who came to my rescue."

In our short conversation, my friend gave me food for thought. There was a lot to learn and a lot of reality in his observation of God's work in man's life. First, to agree with him, our perception of God's work could be deceiving in many ways. There are those who do not believe in the existence of God. They say things like, if there is a God, so good and mighty, why is it that there is so much evil in the world? Others demand physical evidence to prove His existence.

These arguments have their own place; for example, when Job went through his difficulties, he could not understand why God would look on and watch him suffer, after he had done so much for Him. John the Baptist also doubted Jesus' behavior when he was about to be beheaded. These were people who came so close to God that they knew who He was and what He was capable of doing, yet they doubted Him because of their problems. It is easy to doubt God's power and even His existence. We all do that all the time.

I have lived in many communities in different countries around the world and have heard various such stories from time to time. Usually, when people are pushed to the edge, the first thing they do is to doubt God's existence. One such story was about a man, a well-known personality in his community, who had the shock of his life when he lost two of his children within two weeks. Some Christians went to sympathize with him at that sad time. Invoking the name of the Lord, one of the brothers said, "There is one God, and He is all powerful, He is the only one we can always go to when we are in distress." It was as if the brother had started a diatribe. When he was finished, the man replied, "Yes, I know there is one God; if there were another God, he would have pointed out the error of the first God when He was wrong." Well, the scripture says, *"It is only a fool who says there is no God."*

Similar to my friend's example, there are other instances recorded in the Bible where the Lord acted swiftly, miraculously providing for the needs of people. For example, He fed the multitudes with five loaves of bread; He made Moses part the Red Sea for the children of Israel to march through; He raised Lazarus from the dead; He turned water into wine… There are countless numbers of miracles and examples of prompt responses throughout the Bible. In these examples, it is clear to say that my friend had it right. The swiftness of God in solving the problems of His children could be likened to his "athlete suit" metaphor.

Another lesson that could be drawn from my friend's observation is found in the adage that says, "God being so wise, He places His curtains before the future." A curtain as it hangs in a window is used in homes for one or more reasons. It could be used to beautify the home, to reduce or prevent the sun's harmful rays from entering the home or to obscure the view of those both inside and outside the house. There may be other reasons why others use window curtains but here, let's use the latter definition to address the saying above. If God had given us the details of our future—when we will die, be sick, fall into trouble, be sent to jail, be rich, be poor etc.—what would our world look like? Could it be a safer place or the worst place ever? What kinds of decisions would we be likely to make, positive or negative? It is anyone's guess what our world would be like, but I suspect there would be mere anarchy and things would fall apart as Chinua Achebe, one of Africa's renowned writers, puts it.

In Isaiah 55:8-9 the scriptures says: *"'for my thoughts are not your thoughts, neither are my ways your ways,' said the Lord. 'For as the heavens are higher than the earth, so are my ways higher than your ways and my thoughts higher than your thoughts.'"*

In these scriptures, God describes a line of distinction between Him and mankind. We don't get to decide for Him when our problems should be solved or how they should be solved; He does it in His own timing. So, the question of how soon or how late He comes into our life to solve our problems depends on what He wants to achieve. It could be so that our faith can be tested, so that we can learn more about patience, or for a number of other reasons, or the situation could be a question of timing, as it is in Ecclesiastics 3.

The experience of my friend was one of those in which the Lord chose to act swiftly. Like my friend, I saw God's imminent intervention in my wife's illness from the day she fell. January 3rd was one of several days when God demonstrated His swiftness to us once more.

On the previous day, January 2nd, the doctor had given us his lengthy report from his assessment about my wife, which created a cloud of doubts as to whether or not she would be sent to the rehab center. The question of how long it would take was uncertain, but even if she were to go, according to the doctor's report, her recovery was expected to be a lengthy one. Surprisingly, within less than 24 hours, later on January 3rd, we experienced the swiftness of God; His miracle once again graced our day. The requirements to be evaluated on swallowing, to follow commands and to focus, as defined by the doctor, were all met beyond expectation on this day. As God would have it, two of the nurses witnessed the incident that morning.

With a good night's rest, my wife woke up at about 5 A.M. Her eyes were clear; she looked very much awake and relaxed. She turned and tossed for some time. I thought she was in pain, but she was not and I was about to be surprised by what I would hear. About 30 minutes later, she said, "I want to have a shower." I was enthralled and didn't know exactly how to respond. I wanted the nurses or the doctors to hear this. I regretted their absence. None of them were around to see for themselves. I am sure if they were there, the note taking would take a different turn from that point onwards. What I could feel within myself at that moment was actually a great deal of excitement, a spirit of ecstasy.

I went on to call the nurses to help me take my wife to the bathroom to give her a well-deserved shower. As it turned out, this was just the beginning of what was to continue later after her shower. After the shower, at about 6:45 A.M., she began to roll from one end of her tiny bed to another, almost falling off the bed. She managed to roll to the foot of the bed. I asked her, "D.Q., what has happened?" To my amazement, she said in a scruffy tone of voice, "I want to get down." Again, in less than two hours, a woman they said would have a lengthy recovery was now having a full conversation with her husband. As excited as I was, I couldn't allow her to get up; it was something I really didn't need a second thought about; I had to get permission from the nurses confirming that it was safe to do so. Also, because the incision VAC and the PICC line were still attached to her, I needed the nurses' assistance. So, I rang for the nurses to come in to help. Within seconds, one of them came. My wife was still at the foot of the bed in tears, crying to get up. She managed to get her feet down from the bed and knelt down before the bed. This was the first time since December 8th, 2007 that she had rested on other parts of her body—her knees. She had been bedridden throughout that time.

From what I noticed, it appeared that her body had begun recovering and responding to pain. She continued to toss and turn from one side to the other. Just then another nurse came in; it was about time for a shift changeover and the regular assessment was about to take place as well. With two nurses by my side and my wife kneeling before the bed, it was the nurses' decision whether to let her go back onto the bed or to grant her wish. It would be difficult to deny her request, given the effort she was making to recover. So they quickly thought of giving her the opportunity to sit up in the recliner, but to do so, they had to find a way to either remove the PICC line and the feeding tube or attach both to the stand and take it along with her to the recliner, which was about five to ten feet away from her bed. Just then she pointed to the bathroom suggesting that she wanted to use it. I came closer to help take her there. One of the nurses also came to help. From her kneeling position she stood up for about thirty seconds with only me standing by her side. She attempted to walk by herself and did so by taking two steps forward and then stopped. Her feet began to wobble. The wobbling of her feet was a testimony to the fact that after 26 days of being bedridden she was in a weakened condition. We helped her to the bathroom. From the bathroom we held her arms and led her to the recliner. Sitting by herself with her feet rested on the floor for the first time was again another miracle. "What a surprise this morning," said one of the nurses.

As you can see, the brightness of the day in terms of the miracles being displayed was relentless. We had only spent a few hours of the day and already a lot had been achieved. By now I was satisfied with the new developments, even if nothing else would happen for the rest of the day. Like in my friend's story, the day also reminded me of the argument of "the living way," as written in the book, "*The Real Faith for Healing*" by Charles S. Price, edited and rewritten by Harold J. Chadwick. He writes: "In the days of Jesus' earthly walk, the Pharisees cried, 'Lo here is truth' and the Sadducees, in contradiction, said, 'No, it is here.' The Grecian philosophers on the other hand had long proclaimed that they had the truth. Our Blessed Lord, however, silenced them all in His declaration, *'I am the way, the truth, and the life. No man cometh unto the Father but by me.'*"

The argument in the medical world continues in the same vein today when it comes to healing. Most often, when physicians' diagnoses declare their patients not survivable, they may even say, "You have X number of days to live." Some secularists would buy into this view saying yes, the doctors have spoken, and with such consensus it is almost impossible to hear from others what the Lord's position might be.

I would argue that until the chief physician gets the last word, *"I am the way, the truth, and the life,"* any patient is survivable.

At about sunset between 5 and 6 P.M., one of the older nurses came in to see my wife. She had been working with my wife since we were transferred to Level 3300. She wasn't assigned to her directly on this day, but I guess she was told about the day's development. It also appeared that she was on a fact-finding mission. By then my wife was already in bed, having a rest after sitting in the recliner for over 45 minutes during the morning hours. She still appeared calm and very restful. Given what she had seen, the nurse decided to share her story with us. She said, "Twenty-seven years ago, I was very sick for three months and had to go through dialysis (a procedure to remove waste products from the blood of patients whose kidneys no longer function). My doctor told me I had only two days to live, but a few days later a miracle happened and my doctor told me, 'I have nothing to do with this.' Here I am today," she concluded. Due to this statement, I was thankful that more doctors and nurses were beginning to use the word "miracle."

The report from the nurses' assessment done some time that morning says the following: "Patient awake with similar responses/activities as yesterday. No changes—sitting in chair, wound VAC in place; swallow study failed with poor airway penetration/aspiration. Patient seemed to offer continued support to her family. Patient with several family members, appearing to do well. Patient needed a lot of assistance to get back in bed." Another doctor came in later, made his assessment and noted the following: "I saw and evaluated patient, agree with previous notes. Continue to improve. Following commands, some appropriate verbalization with assistance. Wound VAC in place."

The other doctors' and nurses' notes appeared to be slightly different from our experience in the morning, but again, this wasn't anything strange and that did not frighten me any longer. It was my belief that the Lord was now in His "athletic suit" ready to act and prove Himself to doubters. I also believe that He gets the last word, *"I am the way, the truth, and the life,"* and I had no doubt that my wife was well on the way towards healing. With the many friends and family members visiting on this day and witnessing those signs of recovery and God's miracle, there was joy, laughter and semi-celebration in the room. Other church members came to pray with us and encourage us. For the rest of the day, my wife chose to sit up instead of lying in bed, as had been the case until now. But rather than moving her back and forth to the recliner, we adjusted her bed in a reclined position so that she had the chance to sit up as long as she wanted.

JANUARY 4th, 2008

"'I will lead the blind by ways they have not known, along unfamiliar paths I will guide them; I will turn the darkness into light before them and make the rough places smooth. These are the things I will do; I will not forsake them,' says the Lord."

Isaiah 42:16

JANUARY 4TH WAS ANOTHER INTERESTING day. On that day I found out about an amazing event that had happened in my absence when I had gone to work some days ago. By January 4th I had resumed work with Core Services as a supervisor for about a week and half. My schedule ran from 3 to 9 P.M., which was the part-time schedule I had arranged with my office to afford me some extra time with my wife at the hospital. My father-in-law was a great help in running this schedule. Just before he left for home (Africa), some of our community friends had been coming to fill in at times when he needed to go home to take a rest. Again, our friend, Younger, was one of those always there to help. She worked for the same hospital but at a different location at Northside. She was scheduled on the first shift and got off at 3 P.M. She was available between 4 P.M. and 9 P.M. to help on her workdays and came in during the morning hours whenever she was off.

As early morning hours of January 4th arrived, at 4:15 A.M., there were signs that we would be launching into another day full of good news. My wife was awake at 4:30 A.M. but still lying in bed with her eyes open, staring at the ceiling and walls of her bedroom. With my recliner only a few feet away, a position from which I could see her and quickly reach out to assist if there was a need to do so, I was comfortable watching her, since she didn't appear to be distressed. Moments later D.Q. turned around onto the other side of the bed where my recliner was. When our eyes met, I didn't want to be seen to be neglectful, so I quickly got up from my recliner and rushed over to her to find out what she wanted. I asked, "D.Q., are you okay?" She said, "I want to have a shower."

This was the second day in a row that she had asked for a shower just about the same time. Her peaceful appearance and the request to have a shower were a ray of hope on a glorious day we were about to begin. This moment meant a whole lot to me, even more than the first time she had said it. But it was also a day when I needed to convince the doctors to break down the skepticism they continued to have about my wife's swallowing evaluation that seemed not to be ending. Without hesitation, I ran out into the hall to call a nurse to assist me. In a few seconds she was there, she disconnected the wound VAC and other tubes to get my wife ready for the shower.

The request to have a shower was not strange; we had been through it on the previous day, but the fact that she repeated her request for a second time was the interesting part. What it really meant to me was that it signaled the beginning of a routine that appeared to be unstoppable. Also, "I want to have a shower" was not the only thing that helped build more confidence that morning, in me as well as the nurses. Later after the shower, the nurse and I would be shocked by what we would hear again from her.

When the shower was over, I told the nurse to change the sheets while I helped my wife get dressed. When we were done, it was time to take her back to bed. Because she chose to walk, two persons were needed—one on each side to help her back to bed for safety reasons. She took a few steps with me and the nurse helped me take her back to the bed. Usually, when she was in bed, we used a lot of pillows to secure both ends of the bed to avoid her falling over in case she became agitated. Remembering to do that, the nurse brought in a couple of pillows. When she was about to start propping my wife up, she watched her intently and said something that inspired us.

Already from the beginning of the day, my confidence had not only increased but I was totally convinced that we had overcome the need to continually reschedule the swallowing test. Postponing the evaluation schedule from one time to another was getting to the point where I was finding it difficult to believe that it was all about my wife not following commands. She had been engaging us in real conversation most of the time in those early morning hours. That morning, as if the Lord were truly in His athletic suit, my wife was ready to convince the doubters beyond reasonable doubt again.

Noticing what the nurse was about to do, my wife said, "Leave it, my husband will do it for me. He is a wonderful man." Being shocked, the nurse responded, "Hmm, okay," with a brilliant smile at my wife. My wife smiled back as well. In her notes the nurse wrote, "Doing amazingly well, went to bathroom with support and had a shower, sat out for an hour, talking sentences now."

Despite all of this, little did I know that even more amazing things had been happening in my absence when I had gone to work some days earlier. Being blissful by what I had witnessed and heard from my wife, I thought I had to share the news with just about anyone who came to visit that morning. As it turned out, Younger, our friend, had a day off from work that day. As was her way, she came in to give us some help. I hadn't seen her for a couple of days. It was about 11 A.M. by the time she arrived. Being one of those people who had been with me since the crisis began, I thought she was the right person to share the story with. After I explained everything that had taken place in the morning, she was as happy as I was, but her body language communicated something different. I didn't want to be judgmental and think that she was only pretending to be happy. What I didn't know was that my story was just enough to remind her of an experience she had had with my wife a few days earlier. After hearing my story, she told me that when I was away from the hospital a few days before, my wife had sent her to go and get one of the nurses to give her some food to eat. With this story and the one I had just told her, there was no doubt my wife was ready for a transfer, but the doctors were still holding us back.

The facts were glaring. She was now communicating in sentences and taking little steps. There was no doubt in my mind that it was now God's time to set a date for full recovery—walking and doing other physical activities. But at this point, the speech therapist had not come to conduct her evaluation. We anxiously waited for her to come and to see what the outcome would be after the evaluation was done.

Finally, at 3:38 P.M., she showed up. She conducted the assessment; it took her about two minutes. In her report, she said the following: "Patient continues to exhibit inconsistent swallow reflex delay (1-5 seconds), cough with thin liquid. Appeared to tolerate pureed texture and nectar/honey thick boluses. Recommend repeats MBS prior to initiation of P.O. (by mouth) to adequately assess swallow safety."

The therapist's report suggested another postponement. Whether the doctors', the nurses' or the therapist's actions were predicated upon delaying my wife's stay at the hospital or not, the situation at this time taught me a lifelong lesson. As I see it, the back and forth with the doctors' decision to suspend the evaluation was a reminder of the fragility of life. In the wake of an accident, for example, whether minor or major, in most cases, what God has given us tends to slip away in the blink of an eye, whether for good or temporarily. In such cases, taking your life back to its fullness is like going through the stages a baby has to pass through from childhood to maturity—learning to sit, crawl, stand up, take a few steps and finally to walk. As normal as my wife was prior to the blood clots, it never crossed our mind by any stretch of imagination that one day such a time would come in our lives when my wife would be tutored to eat, speak, walk or learn everything again. So the mere fact that she was once clinically dead or presumed dead and later became a bit responsive, and then slowly began to open her eyes, exhibit minimum body movement, regaining the strength to talk, but in short sentences only, were all the uphill tasks that are part of the price of recovery. Above all, God being the overseer of every step, we were thankful to be where we were at this juncture. The doctors' delay to move forward with the transfer procedures was just another factor within the progressive pattern of recovery that made for a temporary setback.

As January 4th came to an end, we still had no clue as to when my wife would be transferred for her therapeutic treatment. Our best guess at the end of the day was that unless we could see the paperwork for the transfer, we wouldn't know when it would take place. But the most important event at the end of our day was that the signs my wife continued to show were all pointing in a positive direction. From the level of recovery we had seen in the previous few days it was my assumption that we might not have to employ a physical therapist after all. So we kept our fingers crossed as we waited patiently for each day that followed to unfold.

JANUARY 5th, 2008

SOME REFLECTIONS ABOUT THE PAST. Throughout the crisis, there were times when tears became my companions; there were also other times when uncertainty clouded my judgment and I became faithless. The worst of those days was a period in which an uneasiness stirred in the pit of my stomach, when I was told my wife was clinically dead. Not only that, it was even more horrific when I heard other rumors that she was indeed dead. Reflecting on these days helped me not only to understand the long journey we had taken to be where we were today but also I had been strengthened by the power of prayers from many people and believed without a doubt that a transformation had taken place in me.

At this stage of the crisis there was a complete turn about from the worst-case scenario to a more plausible condition. This level of recovery, as noted in previous daily notes, continued to improve and appeared to have no end in sight until the Lord would finish His work. When I look back, all I see is history—the tears, the uncertainty and misjudgment of my wife's condition. They are now gone and, I believe, gone forever. Now, writing about this story is one thing and the visual images I expect my readers to have as I try to write from my heart as it happened is another. In other words, it is easy to write or read about an event from the past, but it is quite another thing to truly understand how difficult it is to live through the actual experience. All I want you to do is to imagine a friend, a relative or a father, a mother or similar images you may have seen on television and then empathize with me just for a moment. I guess that would help you understand exactly what I am talking about. That experience is one that I do not even wish my enemies to go through.

The Bible says it all. Chapter 3 of the book of Ecclesiastics addresses the issue of time. Verses 1, 3 and 4 are mirror images of time as it was in my experience in this crisis. Here, the Bible says: *"To everything there is a season, and a time to every purpose under heaven; a time to kill and a time to heal, a time to break down and a time to build up; a time to weep, and a time to laugh; a time to mourn and a time to dance."* As God led us through these days, experiencing each moment with all that came with it, one thing was certain. He was going to produce the best result from it. In His words it is said, *"Because God wanted to make the unchanging nature of his purpose very clear to the heirs of what was promised, He confirmed it with an oath. God did this so that... we who have fled to take hold of the hope offered to us may be greatly encouraged"* (Hebrews 6:17-18).

Being encouraged by the restoration of my wife's life by the Lord, I could not agree more as a result of the activities of January 5th as well as the events of previous days. A situation that once appeared like death became a healing;

a life that was broken into pieces where things virtually fell apart—the baby in one place, the mother in another with Dad commuting within the walls of the hospital—was now rebuilding up, with no more tears; laughter had now become the order of the day. And if I were mournful during my wife's death experience, my dancing shoes were now ready to be used. Thank God for January 5th.

I considered January 5th as another day of reassurance. Everything done on that day heavily weighed in the positive direction. The progress notes showed that nothing had significantly changed from the previous day. It further states that, "Patient spoke full sentences, made great strides, wound VAC improved and in place." Other nurses who came later during the day simply agreed with preceding daily entries by their colleagues. My wife also spent more hours sitting on the couch than during previous days and she was more alert and talked a lot with others who came to visit.

The only request we continued to have was the swallowing reassessment and the hitherto unknown date of transfer. At every stage, since that day, we continued to ask for reassessment due to my wife's ongoing complaint about hunger. Intermittently she had been eating Popsicles, ice chips and sometimes drinking pure liquid as a means of preparation for the next assessment. But as each nurse came and listened to our request, we were encouraged to wait for a few more days. The scripture teaches, *"Never be lacking in zeal, but keep your spiritual fervor, serving the Lord"* (Romans 12:11). The joy of redemption in me at this time was much more important than the request for reassessment, but I had to ask about the time for a reassessment to satisfy my wife's ardent desire.

JANUARY 6th, 2008

"God will deliver the needy who cry out, the afflicted who have no one to help."

Psalm 72:12

ON SEVERAL OCCASIONS I HAD DISCUSSED or argued with doctors, nurses and hospital administrators concerning my wife's condition when she was in pain and needed medication to calm her down. Even prior to this, I had rebuked nurses for disclosing her medical condition to those who were not authorized to receive such information. I also sometimes argued with nurses when I thought my wife was receiving the wrong treatment. I had asked whether she could be fed with solid food, as she requested several times. In short, my relationship with the nurses had been bittersweet. It was one in which credibility sometimes came into question where I ignored professional explanations. But there were also many other days when we worked together in harmony, peace and joy. To me such experiences are normal. These things happen when the patients or patients' loved ones become desperate. To their credit, I believe every nurse we came across did what she could do to help.

On the daily assessment sheet, the findings reported on January 6th were no different from the previous ones. It showed that my wife's condition continued to improve. As a specific example, the chart showed the following: under neurological problems identified, where n=no and y=yes, it says: confused, yes; lethargic, no; comatose, no; difficulties arousing, no. Also, the communication assessment was done. Here is the report: slur communication, no; rambling, no; garbled, no and aphasic, no. Everything under respiratory assessment showed no problems. The report also indicated no cardiac problem and no gastrointestinal problems. To me, this was the work of the Lord, saying no to what man thought was a downright death case.

The regular shift changeover report confirmed all of the above findings. Notes taken and reported by the outgoing and incoming nurses agreed with previous findings. The last nurse on the day shift wrote, "I saw and evaluated patient, agree with above. Wound closing well, continues to improve, continue present care."

As a sign of better recovery my wife had begun sleeping through her regular eight hours and requested a shower every morning at the usual time between 5 and 6 A.M. She relentlessly continued to ask for something to eat.

Until now, there had been no appointment for the reassessment. Despite the recovery level, doctors still needed a much better result before any appointment could be made. My wife picked up on what she construed as an unnecessary delay. She became more vocal and demanded the removal of the feeding tube from her nose and vowed never to have it reinstalled. She cried, and became very angry, as I had been with the doctors for delaying her swallowing evaluation. It was at this time that I saw the need to take the back seat while my wife became the driving force, defending and advocating for herself. She was now capable of expressing her desire as to what she wanted and what she did not want.

I realized that at this time we had joined forces in experiencing the crisis together as a couple. I respected her views, more so for being angry about the delay with the test and transfer. I thought that allowing her to speak out for herself made sense because it would be much easier to understand her weariness caused by the postponement. The anger and emotions she expressed showed she was no longer willing to go any further with the waiting. I hoped her demonstration of strong emotions would bring about a quicker resolution to her problems. As it turned out, by the end of that day, the doctors saw the need to hasten the process. She was scheduled for re-evaluation on the next day, January 7th.

That impromptu decision to reschedule her for the long awaited evaluation reminded me of some jokes about hospital administration. One of them says, "We waste time so that you don't have to." The other says, "Don't expect doctors to believe anything you tell them." Wasting time is a common practice in almost all the hospitals that I have visited. Often the patient is told to wait for further observation. While waiting, there are repeated observations carried out and repeated tests done. Whether it is necessary or not, it is a question only the doctors can answer. Patients have no way of knowing what doctors really suspect, that may cause further problems, so when patients are asked to wait, they usually don't pressure the doctors for answers, to their own detriment. That also makes it easier for the doctors to ignore their patients' requests and so they have no way of knowing what their patients think or believe.

In retrospect, thinking about our arguments with the doctors, as we demanded that my wife be tested and transferred, I realize that there is a lot of truth in these jokes. We were in an uphill battle that was not winnable by any easy means, except by the steps my wife had taken and above all by God's intervention. In fairness, there are potential arguments to be made from the doctors' perspective on the subject of delays or long waiting periods. That debate is regrettably not the subject of this book.

For days and weeks my wife requested food. Whatever we said, whether with positive or negative emotion, the doctors found no evidence to believe us. We thought it was God who actually intervened to hasten the schedule for the next day. Even though my wife had some strength to do what she did from morning to evening, we believe she was only a conduit for the success that occurred at the end of the day. We ended the day expecting her to pass the swallowing evaluation scheduled for the next day. That evaluation meant so much to us. Passing it would have led to a decision concerning two things: first, she would have the opportunity to eat solid food. She had begun refusing the milky and watery food they were giving her. So she needed to pass the test for her demands to be met. Secondly, she would also have the chance to be transferred to the next facility to begin her physical and speech therapies. So, even though we were anxious to have all of this done, a lot depended on the test itself. But thankfully, we finally had an appointment.

JANUARY 7th, 2008
BABY TURNED ONE MONTH
MOTHER'S SWALLOW TEST

"He is your God, the one who is worthy of your praise, the one who has done mighty miracles that you yourself have seen."

Deuteronomy 10:21

JANUARY 7TH WAS A MAJOR BREAKTHROUGH. Many things happened on this day that I will never forget. At the beginning of the day there were a few things planned to accomplish. First, it was our son, Baby John's one-month anniversary, as he was born on December 7th, 2007. I had planned to observe this milestone by having his photos taken. Second, we had an appointment scheduled for my wife's re-evaluation of the swallowing test. As far as the day was concerned, these were the items on our agenda. Coincidentally, both of these items were planned for the morning hours. The baby's photo-shoot was at 10 A.M. and the test was scheduled between 11 A.M. and noon.

For the baby's photos, I had planned to take him to a Sears's store. Later, I would drop him off at home with Kabou Nignan, one of my wife's closest friends who had come from Indiana to assist us. I would then go back to the hospital to rejoin my wife and other friends to wait for the test, which was expected to take place before noon.

The baby's photos went as planned. I had several nice photos taken with him to observe his one-month birthday. Born in the 38th week due to his mother's high-risk pregnancy that led to preeclampsia, he weighed four pounds ten ounces at birth. At the time of the photo-shoot one month later he weighed six pounds and a few ounces, but appeared a bit smaller in his clothing—looking like a fledgling bird. With the help of Kabou Nignan and the photographer, he was well propped up for the photo that made him look more like a seven-pounder. After the photo-shoot I dropped him off and went on to the hospital. We also planned for Kabou and the baby to join us at the hospital later during the day so that his mom could see him on his important day.

Appearing more peaceful, calm and confident, my wife was sitting with friends when I arrived. It was about 11:30 A.M. and the nurses had not turned up yet for the test. Being a bit unsure about the outcome of the test, my wife asked Michelle Gayechuway, "Do you think I will pass the test?" Michelle is another friend, more like a sister who had come from Texas to help. Their friendship goes back to their church in Africa. Their relationship is a story that would take a book-length to explain. But Michelle, like my wife, is a woman with strong faith in God. In her response to my wife's question she said, "There is nothing God cannot do." She went on to reassure my wife that God would see her through.

At about 12:30 P.M. we were still waiting; no one had showed up for the test. Being curious, everyone that stopped by that morning for a visit was still willing to go the extra mile to wait and find out the outcome of the test before leaving. They were all enthused by my wife's level of improvement. They chose to wait as long as it would take for her to be called in for her test. Recounting what she had been through, one of our friends said, "God is wonderful to have you sitting here today." She went on to revisit everything she could remember that had happened to my wife, just to appreciate God more. As if she were giving a prepared response, my wife said to our amazement, "Thank God, I am free at last." She smiled brilliantly after making that statement. As I watched her speak those words, I muttered to myself, saying, *Yes indeed, you are truly free at last, no longer in the bondage of the enemies; the Lord has done His work.*

I believe the expression; "Thank God, I am free at last" is not commonly used. For a woman, whom many, including the doctors, thought would have a neurological problem if she survived, to mention these words in response to a statement from someone that prompted such a response was significant. I didn't think these words were coming from the mouth of a previously clinically dead person. It made me endlessly marvel at the work of the Lord. This statement fed directly into the heart of the suffering she had been through. I guess it was a timely coincident for her friend to unintentionally prompt her to speak these words on the day that she was scheduled to have a test for swallowing, which was a major move in her recovery process. It was a second major occurrence of the day in addition to the baby's photo-shoot. I guess it was a shocker that made its way into the minds of the visitors where it would indelibly remain for a long time.

At about 1 P.M. we received word that there would be a further delay before my wife would be called in for the test. According to the information given, there were several other patients in line before her that were scheduled for the same test that day. Our estimated waiting time was between two to three hours. With the time being 1 P.M., it meant it would be 4 or 5 P.M. before she would finally get to see the doctor. It was a day we longed for and we were a bit disappointed, but we had no choice but to wait. Just then the physical therapist showed up. He was normally there in the mornings, so we were surprised to see him at about 1:30 P.M.

When the therapist arrived, something happened that touched everyone's heart who was waiting with us—the doctors', nurses' and the many friends'. Throughout the morning, my wife had only walked to the bathroom twice with my assistance. She had been sitting on the couch ever since. The distance from the couch to the bathroom was about seven to ten feet. Walking this distance with my assistance had become a normal procedure for her, but she could not yet to do it by herself. With the therapist, she was expected to do more than just walk to the bathroom. He began with the regular routine: "Show me two fingers; wiggle your toes; show me your left foot; your right foot; your right hand; your left foot; stand up; sit down…" She managed to pass the preliminary physical test with the therapist. He then asked, "Can you walk with me?" My wife answered, "Yes."

Here was where the neck-stretching, eyebrow-raising, and the most dazzling event was about to happen. The journey he had in mind was a long hallway on the same floor at Level 3300. I do not know the exact length, but it was estimated to be approximately 150 feet long. We stepped out into the hallway to see her walk with the therapist. Because that would be her first time to do this, none of us was sure whether she could go far enough. When she got out into the hallway, I remember there were a lot of people standing around watching. There were doctors, nurses, many of whom had been involved in her treatment. There were also some visitors who came to visit other patients and out of curiosity decided to stand by and watch. We all stood ready to watch what we didn't know was about to happen.

To our amazement, she took the first step, the second, third and went on to walk the entire distance with no difficulty but with lots of smiles and a lot of thumbs up from those watching. With the therapist's assistance holding her hand, she was able to complete the second major physical test.

"Wow!" one of the supervisors exclaimed. He happened to be a nurse who was also involved with my wife's treatment. He said further, "This has to be something beyond us." He went on to say, "I was home last night thinking about your wife's condition, just to come today and see this happening." It was a breathtaking moment as we stood watching another miracle take place before our very eyes. My wife was still full of smiles as we all walked back into the room.

The supervisor's statement, "It has to be something beyond us," underscores the possibility that it was beyond their ability to fully restore my wife to normalcy and that it had to be someone superior. And to me that superior being was God. It was His miracle that I thought had taken place ever since day one of the incident and that continues to manifest and make those less likely to believe His work to confess the errors of their ways. I was even more gratified that while we were yet to do the swallow test, He continued with His miracles as a testimony to His greatness.

So far, on this day alone we had experienced three important events: the baby's photo-shoot, the surprising statement, "Thank God, I am free at last" and now her first long distance walk along the corridor of Level 3300. As you can see, January 7th was truly a day full of events and amazement, but the last major event, the test, was yet to come. Whether we were to end this day with complete success depended on the outcome of the test. A positive result from the test would lead to a complete removal of the feeding tube. So our last hope was in God, believing that He would guide us through the swallowing test.

It was around 2:30 P.M. and we were still waiting. I was scheduled to work each day from 3 to 9 P.M. In 15 minutes I would be leaving my wife in the care of our friends and other relatives. I planned on keeping in touch with her every 30 minutes from work. By 4 P.M. I called from work. They told me she had finally been taken for the test. It took several more minutes after many calls to the hospital to hear that she was back from the testing center. I was anxious to know the outcome, but at the same time apprehensive about the result. But I had to call anyway. I called one of our friends for the result. Gleefully, she shouted, "Your wife made it!"

My heart felt cool as never before. "Okay," I said, "I will call back later." It was only about 5 P.M. and I had been on the job for two hours. I wanted to call in to go and see my wife but I couldn't. It would take the next four to five hours before I could leave. But I went through the rest of the workday with excitement and managed to finish work at 9 P.M. to get to the hospital.

Arriving at the hospital at 9:30 P.M., I found that my wife was already asleep. I guess the activities of the day had tired her out and caused her to go to bed early. But some faithful friends were still waiting for me. When I looked around the room, I could see some dishes. It was strange; I was not used to having dishes in there. I was told that after the test, the doctors allowed them to feed her with some light food to begin with. So, a friend brought some soup from home. She ate as much as she could. I had every reason to be thankful to God for the day. Later I met with one of the nurses to chat over the events of the day. She was so happy and felt like everyone else did. It was amazing to see all that took place in one day.

The progress notes turned in later indicate the following: "MBS completed, recommend regular texture diet with thin liquids; patient alert and communicating appropriately; lying in bed, making good movement; improving daily. Patient resting, feeling better, responding well to command as before." On the daily assessment data sheet everything under neurological problems was checked no, suggesting no problems found. Also, under extremities decrease range of motion without symmetry of strength, it was reported 5 for normal and there was no respiratory problem identified as well. Here is the summary of the findings:

"Reason for exam, dysphagia, brain injury, abnormal Modified Barium Swallow. Findings: Modified Barium Swallow—thin nectar and honey-thickened liquids as well as pudding were all administered. All showed premature loss, but there was never any evidence of airway penetration or aspiration. Chewed fruit and cracker were tolerated within functional limits. Patient shows significant improvement in her swallowing function."

Ending the day on such a positive note, it was most likely that we would soon hear the doctors discussing the possibility of a transfer to another facility for the continuation of therapeutic treatment. As far as we were concerned, there was nothing to worry about any more. But given our experiences in the past, as we looked forward to the next day, we weren't too sure what to expect, but I was especially grateful that we had crossed the greatest hurdle, the swallowing test.

Paul wrote in 2 Timothy 1:12: *"I know whom I have believed, and am convinced that He is able to guard what I have entrusted to him for that day."* Like Paul, we had entrusted our day and the rest of the time of recovery to the Lord. Whatever He would lead the doctors to tell us the next day, we knew that His judgment would never be wrong, He would lead us in the right direction as He had done from the beginning. For the first time in many days my wife and I slept soundly that night without any worries about what the next day would bring.

JANUARY 8ᵗʰ, 2008
ONE MONTH OF HOSPITALIZATION

"Get rid of all bitterness, rage and anger, brawling and slander, along with every form of malice. Be kind and compassionate to one another, forgiving each other, just as in Christ God forgave you."

Ephesians 4:31-32

LOOKING BACK TO THE PREVIOUS DAY, January 7th, the memory of all the good things that had happened was still fresh. Given the tremendously exciting moment of Daniella's improvement, there was every reason to forego all bitterness, rage and anger about the delay of the swallowing evaluation. It was finally done and our expectation was met and there would be no more waiting. The doctors and the nurses had had their way, but the Lord was finally in control of it all.

While we expected more good news each day concerning my wife's recovery, it was important to remember one other day and its impact upon us. That day was December 8th, 2007. January 8th, 2008 was exactly one month since the awful day of the first critical event. The nurses who came in that day and knew that my wife could now talk, walk and eat, marveled at what they called "her speedy recovery." Many of them told us stories upon stories about similar situations that had left other patients either dead or cognitively disabled or paralyzed. Every time we thought of December 8th, it reminded us of that chilling experience. Looking forward, all we could see were the blessings of the Lord. The lesson of blessings was the reason why we were going from one anniversary to another—a back-to-back observation of two important days in our family life. More importantly, what many thought was an unlikely journey came to a conclusion by the end of the first month; my wife was by then well enough to realize what had happened to her. It had now become a story we could tell and joyously give praises to God. Apart from prayers and thanks giving planned on that day, we made no decision to celebrate in any shape or form, except for taking the baby to the hospital to visit with his mom for a while on this day.

She started the new day on her new regular diet. Each one of our several friends wanted to bring something to eat. Before the first five hours of the morning ended, our tiny hospital room was crammed with all sorts of food items from friends in addition to the ones prepared by the hospital. She could not eat much of the food since she had just gotten off a liquid diet. The body, especially the esophagus, had to adjust to the new food texture before she could eat more.

On this day we were even more eager to hear from the doctors about her transfer, but until mid-day we had not heard from them regarding that aspect.

Another thing we were hoping would be removed before her transfer was the wound VAC. That too was doing pretty well according to her OBGYN, but they told us that the final decision would be made before the transfer. They had previously discovered that there was an infection within the wound but it had been combated with some antibiotic. We were also told it had been cured.

The physician's progress notes thus far indicated no new problem or any particular reason for concern; it included the information they received from me that she had slept well during the night. The report also states that she was on a regular diet with no respiratory distress; husband at bedside; resting in bed; no pain; tolerating diet well. Also, the daily assessment data report showed that there were no neurological problems identified. The Extremities Disease Range of Motion without Symmetry of Strength shows 4 for good and 5 for normal; Respiratory Problems identified also shows no negative result and no cardiac problems identified. On eating, it reports that there were no difficulties in chewing. Swallowing, aspiration precautions, head of bed elevated 30 degrees and no tube feeding.

We were now convinced that we were headed for another period of recovery—a recovery that would not necessarily require a lot of medication but would be treated therapeutically. The question of what would be needed and how we would get through it was a burden that we thought the Lord would carry for us. The scripture teaches, *"Cast your cares on the Lord and He will sustain you; He will never let the righteous fall."*

By the end of that day I had to go to work again. In my absence some doctors stopped by and left a message that the plan for the next day, which was January 9th, was to possibly transfer Daniella to rehab to continue her therapy. There was no specific time set but they were almost certain that a transfer was possible.

JANUARY 9th, 2008
TRANSFERRED TO REHABILITATION CENTER

"God is able to make all grace abound to you, so that in all things at all times, having all that you need, you will abound in every good work."

2 Corinthians 9:8

JANUARY 9th, AS YOU WILL SOON READ, BECAME the date of the discharge from the hospital to Rehab. Center—a branch of the hospital. We were told that the day had finally come, so I knew we weren't going home straight from the hospital, we were only continuing the recovery process in another area. My instinct, however, told me it was all over. My wife was happy as well; she also knew it wouldn't be too long before she would be home with her baby. The Bible instructs us as Christians to hold unto the unchanging hands of the Lord. As you may have already read in the previous chapters, I was wavering between faith and disbelief.

This day was unusual by human standards but we had arrived to this point according to God's will. As part of the discharge process, this report represents the summary of my wife's hospital record. Here is a portion of it:

"Patient is 38 weeks pregnant and, was being followed in high-risk clinic for poorly controlled chronic hypertension and morbid obesity. During her evaluation she was found to demonstrate asymmetric IUGR with growth reduction from the 25th percentile to the 11 percentile in less than a week. During course of her management she always reported good fetal movement without any loss of fluids or vaginal bleeding or any regular contractions. At the time of admission she denied any chest pain, palpitations, fevers, chills, nausea, vomiting or diarrhea. Upon her arrival she was rescanned to confirm breech presentation, was found to be cephalic.

"Induction of labor commenced. During that induction she was having significant cramping and contraction pain and although the family did request an elective C-section at that time, there were no maternal fetal indications to support that. During the remainder of her induction there was lack of progress and stronger consideration was given for C-section. Eventually she began to demonstrate non-reassuring fetal heart tracing. Decision was made at that time based on these indications to perform a primary low transverse cesarean section. Postoperative day 0 she was doing well, up ambulating with no complaints. Postoperative day 1 she experienced a significant bilateral pulmonary embolism requiring code.

"She was coded twice during the morning. Postoperative day 1 was found to have pulseless electrical activity, was resuscitated, taken to ICU. There she remained on a ventilator for several days. She was noted to have limited reassuring CNS status and was suspected of having significant evidence of encephalopathy. However, the patient improved very slowly. She began to be able to breathe on her own. Was given NG tube feedings through the course of her stay. At multiple opportunities the family was offered a PEG tube and trach and declined. Eventually the patient began to speak, initially in her native language and later in English as well.

"At time of discharge she had been ambulatory for several days and it was felt that a rehabilitation center would be best to get her recuperated. During the course of her hospitalization in ICU she experienced 1 episode of wound breakdown with most likely an underlying hematoma beneath the incision. This was expressed and found to be hemostatic. Eventually she began to run fever during the course of her stay and it was treated with multiple antibiotics under the care of infectious disease. After all other sources were ruled out, it was considered that the incision might be the likely etiology of her fever. A small area was opened up within the incision, initially packed with wet and drys and then wound VAC was placed. Aerobic cultures and anaerobic cultures were obtained, and it was found to be positive for vancomycin-resistant enterococcus and the patient was treated with appropriate antibiotics as a result. At the time of discharge patient was doing remarkably well."

This report could have been written differently. It could have been a report with a tragic ending. Looking back, I still felt like a failure on the grounds that my faith wasn't really put to work the way I had understood faith to be. On the outside, many thought I was being faithful, but on the inside I was on and off, wavering between fear and belief. As the scriptures indicate in Hebrews 5:12-14, what was required of me, having been born in Christ for over two decades, was to live my Christian life with maturity, no longer a baby who feeds on milk, but an adult who eats solid food.

As my wife and I stood side by side on this day ready to move out to the next step with smiles and jubilation and renewed hope that our child, Baby John, would grow up in our care, it was God's mercy and grace that brought us to where we were. In my effort to live for Christ, I have had a number of opportunities to teach Bible lessons to both new converts and to adults. Going forward, if I ever again have another opportunity to teach, which I know will happen, there are a lot of readjustments to do. My practical experience tells me that when temptation, trials and tribulations appear before us, our true nature is revealed. That suggests that our life lessons have more to teach us about how we need to approach the things of God. Synthetic experience has its place but being practical pays.

What I learned from this brought me even closer to the Lord. I am reminded best of all of His promises to us: *"Come unto me, all ye that labor and are heavy laden, and I will give you rest. Take my yoke upon you, and learn from me; for I am meek and lowly in heart; and ye shall find rest unto your souls"*

(Matt. 11:28-30). As a human, I was likely to fall prey to fear or temptation. All the Lord wants us to do is to take all of our troubles onto Him, trusting and believing that despite the magnitude of our problems, He will be willing to take up our burdens.

Going forward as His follower, I think it is cautious to say that all glory belongs to Him, the author and finisher of our faith. This said, I also believe that each one of us is different; people grow up in the Lord differently. Some are stronger than others and that speaks about the lesson of faith as well. For me, I believe I have begun another lesson in faith. During the crisis, there were faithful men and women who demonstrated their strong belief and I am thankful to God for them and what they did for my wife and myself.

CHAPTER 5
NORTHSIDE REHABILITATION CENTER

THERAPEUTIC TREATMENT

"Blessed is the man who perseveres under trial, because when he has stood the test, he will receive the crown of life that God has promised to those who love Him."

James 1:12

OUR DAYS AT THE REHABILITATION center were different. Here my wife was vocal, she had the chance to speak out about what she wanted or did not want. She could tell me, or the nurses, if she felt any pain. She could walk to the bathroom by herself, sometimes with minimal assistance from the nurses or me. To help us understand what was expected at the rehab, on our arrival a nurse told me that patients at that center were considered to be people who were on their way to discharge, but required a few more finishing touches. In much more clearer terms she said, "They are expected to be helpful in doing little chores for themselves." So, with my wife's recent activities, I was not surprised she was ready for the center. We were in the right place, I thought to myself.

She was transferred on January 9th. She would be finally discharged to go home once she had gone through all of the physical and speech therapies successfully. There were a few things they needed to work on, such as her speech and physical exercises—walking and other types of physical activities. So the question of when she would get through all of this remained open-ended. When she finally started her activities, each day between about 8 and 9 A.M., a therapist would show up and take her to the gym for an hour of exercise, walking the distance, which took about three minutes. The speech therapist on the other hand came in only twice and felt my wife didn't need her services any longer. My wife had greatly improved, her voice was clear and she spoke in longer and understandable sentences. She was literally communicating well enough to know that she really didn't need a therapist's help.

Truly, the days at the rehab were different, but encouraging. When I looked back to two or three weeks earlier, I realized a complete change had taken place. Days before there were many questions that I could not hold back and I kept asking the doctors or nurses, such as, *"How long do you think it will take to get this problem treated?"* or *"What is the major problem you think she really has now? For such a problem, how long is the recovery period?"* or *"Will she regain everything if she does recover?"* To these questions I received answers I didn't want or expect to hear. Sometimes the closest the doctors would come to answering these questions in the affirmative would be to say, "It will take some time," or "I don't know," or "Going home depends on how fast she responds to treatment." I realized later that I wanted things to go my way. All I wanted was nothing short of my wife's speedy recovery. At the same time I blended faith with doubt. I wasn't too sure, especially considering what I kept hearing from the doctors. The doctors had not entertained the idea of recovery to begin with. Perhaps they didn't want to commit any falsehood to please me but chose to speak from their professional standpoint.

With two people thinking from opposite viewpoints and the only one that could bring an end to the uncertainty was the one who lay prostrate before them between life and death and had no contribution to make but to submit to any decision that would come from the Lord was the most disheartening situation I had ever witnessed. At the rehab center my wife began to ask those same questions but in different ways: "When will I go home? I am all right, what kind of treatment do I still need?" In addition to those questions she also began to say things like, "I need to go home to be with my baby; I am missing my baby." Sometimes in the morning when we woke up, she would ask me, "Daddy, where is John?, I need him. Are we going home today?"

On our arrival at the rehab center, we were not told how long we would be there. The only thing I remember was that before we left the hospital we were told we would be at rehab for about two weeks or a little more depending on her pace of recovery. Based on this, I could not answer my wife's question as to when she would be discharged; all I could say was exactly what we were told, that it would depend on her level of recovery.

But this wasn't the answer she was expecting. Every time I gave her this answer, she became even more irritated. Although she was irritated by my answers, the irritation itself was a positive emotion. Asking and getting emotional about her situation demonstrated that she was relating to her fighting spirit she had exercised even when she could not talk, walk and do anything. She did all this to shake off the illness.

Before the day of discharge came, as the days went on at the rehab, she would be more irritated by other factors. Because she could see clearly now and understand the difference between good and bad, she began to require some privacy, so being in a congested room full of people, she began to react to some behaviors that she couldn't respond to two or three weeks earlier.

When it comes to visitations, the influx of visitors that came in on a daily basis to see her was countless. They had come in every single day in large numbers during the one-month she had spent at the hospital. Those visitations continued at rehab. From the beginning she had no control over the inflow of people. She was unconscious. At that point I had to be cautious and graceful in dealing with the issue. The fact that people had to take time off to come and see us was encouraging. It is often said, "When you fall sick or are in trouble, those who come to see you are people to remember." But massive visitations create their own problems, especially in a hospital setting. As noted in my previous daily notes from ICU 2600 Level, the crowd was so enormous that the nurses became concerned about privacy and their ability to freely administer services. There was no space for any movement in the room. I was forced to authorize the nurses to put a notice on the door in order to help streamline the list of visitors. To this day, there are some of those friends that are still annoyed at me for preventing them from doing what they love to do—being there for a friend, a sister and a fellow Christian.

To some extent, I felt guilty having to prevent someone's intended goodwill toward my family. Perhaps reaching out to the sick is in itself a sermon. Jesus once confronted the disciples when he said: *"Then shall the king say unto them on His right hand, come ye blessed of my father, inherit the kingdom prepared for you from the foundation of the world. For I was hungry, and you gave me meat: I was thirsty, and ye gave me drink: I was a stranger and ye took me in: naked and ye clothed me, I was sick and ye visited me, I was in prison and ye came to me"* (Matthew 25:34-37). The scripture also says, *"No one has ever seen God; but if we love one another, God lives in us and His love is made complete in us"* (1 John 4:12). Later, as I was moved by the influx of these friends, many of whom were Christians, I realized that it was this kind of sermon each of these people was preaching. At the rehab center the story remained the same; the visitations were unstoppable. Friends were happy to see my wife recovered and therefore wanted some time with her. One nurse came to me and said, "You have too many visitors; I think we have to move you into a bigger room to be able to accommodate you."

Such an emotional outbreak of love was irresistible. In spite of my previous decision to streamline the list back at the ICU 2600 Level, coming to the rehab center, I reconsidered my decision for her to have more time with her friends. But little did I know that my actions would be seen later as an encroachment on my wife's rights. As my wife became very conscious at rehab, she wanted to be by herself. I thought her desire was not out of selfishness, but that the many weeks of being bedridden and the confinement in hospital had created the discomfort. I remember telling her one day that I had arranged for a few friends to stay with her when I was due to go to work. Her response was, "Daddy, I want to be by myself; I do not want anyone to baby-sit me." Part of what added to her frustration with many visitors was that at times some of the little ones would come by and put the TV on so loudly that she would become agitated. It seemed she had had enough of that and needed to be by herself.

We ended the first week at rehab with a lot of improvements. But there were other major things we still had to contend with. Due to the nature of what she had gone through, physical and speech therapy was not the end of her recovery journey. I had to take on other duties. When it came to putting on clothes, she had no clue where and how to begin. She could barely tell which was the wrong or right side of the shirt or pants. Sometimes, she didn't remember whether or not she needed to sit down or to stand up to put her pants on. Fastening the buttons was another struggle. She couldn't match the right button to the right hole. Phone numbers, her social security number, her birth date and virtually anything that has to do with numbers or dates were all gone from her memory. She also found it hard to use a spoon to eat. Everything would be wasted on the floor by the time the spoon had reached her mouth. I had to feed her each time the meal was ready. At times when I was doing all of these things for her, she would cry like a baby and would ask me, "Daddy, do you think I will be okay again?" The only assurance that I could give her was to say, "Look back and see what God has done for you and count your blessings. If the Lord was able to give you life, there is nothing He cannot do to complete what He had started. These moments took place privately between us when everyone was gone and we were by ourselves. I would ask her to join me to take a few moments to appreciate God for His work and to stop any doubts. But what I also remembered during this time was an adage from a friend that, "When climbing a hill, the most difficult thing is the first step along the way." So was the situation with my wife; it was one day at a time, as it had been in the past.

By the second week, she was spending time relearning and memorizing her parents' phone numbers in Africa, since they were the main callers that she wanted to talk with. I purchased a phone card and showed her how to use the toll-free numbers and the pin numbers and then she would dial the number to her parents. It was a tough beginning towards normalcy but we worked through it slowly as the days went on at rehab.

Midway during the second week, she got serious about going home. She no longer wanted to stay at the hospital. The wound VAC that had been causing one of the delays was no longer a problem; it had been removed and the incision scar was closed. The physical therapist was not needed any more. His schedule with her was twice or three times a week. When I questioned the nurses regarding her discharge, I was told that she was mainly staying on for further observation. But there were additional possibilities too. For example, I was told that home health care would be required if she were discharged prematurely. As I was making these arrangements, little did I know that my wife's mind was made up and set to go home and nothing could change it. On Thursday of the second week, at about 9 A.M., her parents called from Africa to check up on her. We discussed the option of home health care treatment if she insisted on going home. That option did not sit well with her parents. They wanted her to be patient and stay at the rehab center for a while. We ended our phone conversation and I left to go to work. It was time for me to go to work. My schedule remained the same—3 to 9 P.M. A couple of friends showed up to visit when I was about to leave. They promised to be there until I came back in the evening. I was shocked when I received a call at 4:30 P.M. from the rehab center informing me that my wife was ready to go home. I asked to speak to a nurse on duty and the phone was handed over to her. She told me it was okay for her to leave but as discussed earlier, the home health care services would follow up. The nurse went on to explain the various services offered by the home care staff. From her explanation I realized that there was only a slight difference between the home services and the rehab or hospital care. Also, because I had been trained to take care of most of her routine treatments by now, such as medication administration and the dressing of the wound which was almost gone at the time, I was okay with the decision to let her go home. After my discussion with the nurse on the phone, within about 30 minutes I called back to the rehab to find out if she had left. I was told they had left to go home.

Our little family was indeed about to experience more inevitable changes. For the first time in almost two months, I would be going home directly from work without going to the hospital. And my wife would be sleeping by her baby's side for the first time since his birth. Baby John would have both his mother and father in the same room day and night. We three would be able to bond together in love and reach out to touch each other when needed. It would be a joyous moment to experience, but what lay ahead was unknown, as the recovery could still take many turns.

CHAPTER 6
FINAL DISCHARGE

HOME HEALTH

"Prepare your minds for action; be self-controlled; set your hope fully on the grace to be given you when Jesus Christ is revealed."

1 Peter 1:13

DURING MY WIFE'S LAST DAYS AT THE rehab center she showed no sign of having a peaceful and gentler demeanor towards ongoing issues. It wasn't because the nurses and doctors or the therapists were not giving her the treatment she needed or that she wasn't receiving a healthy dose of friendship from our friends that came round, but rather she had been exhausted by the unexpected prolonged period she had to spend in hospital. One could literally tell she had been driven to the end of her tether by the gloom and agitation expressed on her face, in her language and her behavior, both of which increased by the day. Once she became aware of what was happening, all she wanted was to get away and be home with her baby.

It was indeed a feeling of nostalgia for familiar things: the neighborhood, family, friends, house, and even the bed and all that provides grace and happiness in a family setting. My wife's main concern was for her child; she longed for her baby.

The sense of reassurance and sanctuary you get around familiar things and people is by itself therapeutic in nature. Some nurses understood her plight. She became so hyper and appeared depressed, wishing to go home. They believed it would be very helpful in Daniella's final recovery process if she went home and began minimum routines with her baby to experience normal life once again. In addition, because the only kind of treatment left was the administration of medications and periodic therapeutic treatment as noted earlier, most nurses deemed it vital to let her have her wish to be finally discharged to go home.

At home, she was happy and I was also happy, even though she was discharged prematurely. Being home was a sign that we had returned to normalcy in some respect. On the other hand, it was unknown as to what to expect during the many days ahead. We were hopeful, though, that it was all over and that she would not have to go back to the hospital for any more treatments. The assistance of home health care nurses was an added advantage. Again, friends poured in and out on a daily basis, celebrating her recovery at home.

In addition to the home health care nursing services, we also employed the services of a specialist. His job was to check on her blood, making sure that it was thinned to a level where she would not experience any clots. At the hospital she was on Coumadin. When she was discharged, she remained on this medication. The doctor advised her to continue with it until further notice. When her new specialist was told about it, he decided to continue it as well. After a week of home health care nursing services, an evaluation was conducted. The result showed that she needed no further services at home, so they were stopped. With the home health care services gone, we were only left with her specialist for further attention and consultation. She was to see him at least once a week and if there were any concerns she could see him more often. On her first visit, he saw that everything appeared to be normal. He asked her to continue with the same dosage of Coumadin that she had been taking at the hospital. Surprisingly, on the second visit, the doctor saw that the blood had thickened a little. As a precaution, he increased the dosage. A few days later, my wife started experiencing the following:

Slurred speech (dysarthria)
Light-headedness
Feeling weak
Confused
Vision problems
Loss of appetite
Chills, even if the heat was turned on.

One morning she got up and felt very weak and complained about having blurred vision. A friend was with us that morning when it happened. She suggested that we take her to the emergency room for a check up. We did and after several hours of various types of tests, they found nothing that may have led to the problems. The emergency room (ER) was part of the same hospital where she had spent those several weeks earlier. We were blessed to see one of the nurses that had helped take care of her at the time. She provided the doctors with more information that in turn helped them to complete all the tests they thought could yield some useful information. But to their amazement they found nothing relating to any of the previous issues that had occurred during her hospitalization. She was discharged a few minutes after the test results were examined.

On the following day, I thought it wise to take her back to her doctor, the specialist, to be sure that we would not again be taken in by surprise. After explaining what had happened, he confirmed that her symptoms were the side effects of Coumadin. Understanding that Coumadin is an anticoagulant (blood thinner) that reduces the formation of blood clots, we had a choice to stop the medication or continue with it. That choice was a hard one— it could actually be a choice between life and death. That means that we could have either disregarded the slurred speech and continued with the Coumadin to avoid another blood clot or stopped the Coumadin and faced the consequences.

That visit to the doctor's office provoked a whole host of questions we had to ponder. Among those were: *Should we go with the doctor's position and continue with the high dose of Coumadin or should we stop and find alternative means to thin her blood? If our choice would be to find alternative means, what is the possibility that we would succeed? Or, How long would she be on the blood thinner if we decided to go with the doctor's advice? How long would it take us to come up with a decision to stop or continue the blood thinner? Could there be future pregnancies, since we still intended to have more children? If a pregnancy were possible, how about the child's health, being born of a mother on blood thinner?*

It was a bewildering time in what was supposed to be the final stage of my wife's recovery, a period that should have been spent in joy. While it looked likely that my wife was not going to be hospitalized again, we certainly had to find lasting solutions to those questions. There was no other way around it. We had to squarely face these issues.

It was clear that the doctor was unwilling to compromise his decision to reduce the dosage. At that moment we also could not come up with a decision as to whether or not my wife should continue with the medication. We went home depressed. My wife was very concerned, especially with the quality of her voice. She did not want to stutter. But I was reminded of something the doctor had told us on the first day of our visit with him. We were given a list of dos and don'ts regarding what types of food she should be eating and those not to eat. At that time, she was also told to avoid using sharp objects like knives, needles and the like. A cut that may lead to profuse bleeding, he said, could cause a potential problem and could lead to more blood clots. Subsequently, we began to dig deeper in search of more information as to the types of food to avoid. If that would help, it could give us an idea of what to do going forward.

On our previous visit to the doctor's office, one of the nurses provided us with some information on the types of food to eat in moderation. Being on a blood thinner you should not eat so much of these foods, she said. She advised that to be on the safe side, it was better to completely avoid them. The list includes the following foods:

Spinach, or any type of green leaves
Kale
Broccoli
Brussel sprouts
Cabbage

According to her, these foods are rich in vitamin K and could play a major role in the formation of blood clots if a lot of them were to be consumed at one sitting or over the course of several meals.

It was becoming more difficult, especially when you start getting a lot of restrictions on what to eat and what not to eat. Having such restrictions, freedom seems to be taken away and choices become limited. These precautions could have been the first convincing evidence that something grave might be waiting for us ahead if we were not careful with our choices.

At the rehab center these realities were never anything we had to contend with; in fact, little was said at the time about the recommended dos and don'ts. Perhaps the lack of emphasis on the do's and don'ts at the rehab might have contributed to my wife's somewhat hasty decision to discharge herself early. They managed her health, from the food she ate to the physical exercises she needed. We didn't have to worry about anything. She never had any symptoms that she was now having. But after less than three weeks at home, we were faced with this new reality.

When it comes to food preparation I was not the right guy to depend on entirely. I am not good at it. My wife is aware of that weakness of mine. During those normal days prior to her hospitalization, she never allowed me to do any kind of cooking, even though I had volunteered my services several times. Sometimes, when I managed to cook in her absence, my food would end up being trashed after days of being left in the refrigerator without anyone attempting to take a share of it. Sometimes to be nice to me, my wife would choose to re-cook the same food to give it a better taste in order to grace my effort. During the time when she wasn't strong enough to prepare anything for herself she had to rely on the efforts of others who would sometimes prepare recipes she would like.

The question then became whether or not it was a regrettable decision to leave the rehab center prematurely. We began to worry a little bit, but there was still some room for hope. In terms of food, my wife still had more choices but, as mentioned earlier, the major hurdle was the decision whether to stop the Coumadin or continue with it. We were yet to get there. It would be a tough choice to make, so we had to be extra careful. Dealing with the problem of Coumadin was really an uphill task considering what was involved. The deeper we went in seeking more information about it, the more difficult it became to understand this medication we knew little about, yet we continued to investigate the repercussions if we were to take up our option of avoiding it.

In our search for more answers, we learned from a report on *mybloodthinner. org* that Coumadin comes second only to chemotherapy drugs as far as having the highest risk of serious complications is concerned. Also, in a Q&A section from another website, *myoclinic.com*, in response to the question whether or not there was any harm in using Coumadin for long-term treatment, Sheldon G. Sheps M.D. provided the following response: "For most people with single episode of deep vein thrombosis (DVT), treatment with full-dose blood thinners is usually for only a limited time. Taking high dose of Warfarin (Coumadin) for a longer period of time is only recommended for people who are at high risk of developing blood clots that could cause a heart attack, stroke or pulmonary embolism." As for the question relating to people with a single episode of DVT that requires a limited time usage, it created another question for us. Was my wife in this category, and if so, was she truly safe from any danger of another episode? Most reports seemed to suggest that indeed she was.

A Food and Drug Administration report, released in August of 2007 on Coumadin says, "A person's genes 'encode' enzymes and differences in the sequence of a gene can cause differences in enzyme activities or sensitivity." The report notes that is why different people process the same drug differently. The report further states that one-third of patients receiving Warfarin metabolize it quite differently than expected. Research had shown, the report continues, that some of the unexpected response to Warfarin depends on a patient's variants in the genes CYP2C9 and VKORC1. But, as Lary Lesko points out in the report, more studies are needed to explore the precise starting dose for those patients.

I suspect that these differences, even though not yet finally confirmed, may have had an impact in my wife's situation in the way she responded to the drug three weeks after her discharge from the rehab center. Although nothing in her family background indicates any blood clots or treatment with Warfarin, her response demonstrated weak resistance, evidenced by the side effect of the drug, as noted. Despite these warning signs, almost every report cited above concluded that, "The benefits outweigh the risks."

After we had combed through all the options, it became time to make a decision. At this time, any decision arrived at would need to be functional. We had been flexible enough to consider other voices on what the outcome might be. Through the search, we had also exposed ourselves to another alternative by asking more doctors, friends with experience in this area and through the various website sources mentioned. From a scholarly viewpoint, we were well on the way to making an informed decision, having gathered enough facts on the drug. On my part, I advised my wife to continue with her medications (Coumadin), as the doctor had suggested. I thought that her recovery was much more important to me than the quality of her voice. My wife had a different take on the issue despite the information we had obtained from our research on how fatal it would be to abruptly stop taking her medications. She took a decision that I think was based on "a leap of faith."

A leap of faith is not necessarily a bad approach in the decision making process, especially for those within the Christian community. It is one of the ways to please God. The Bible teaches that without faith it is impossible to please God. On the other hand, a leap of faith is a two-way street. It could be negative or positive, depending on the choice made, especially when faith in God is not a factor.

After my wife and I had gone through every piece of information we could find to help us make a decision on what to do next, we found ourselves at a crossroad between two equally important decisions about a life or death issue. As I noted, my choice was to stick with the drug (Coumadin) for fear that we might find ourselves faced with another episode of blood clots. But as Dr. Mike Maroon said, speaking on the topic of a leap of faith, "The leaps we make in our lives, come in the face of some of our biggest fears. For such leaps," he adds, "force us to face our fears head-on and reassess our values and beliefs." He notes that when you make a leap of faith in life, it instantly increases your awareness to a new sense of reality. This, he points out, allows you to constantly improve every aspect of your life.

After I had made my suggestion to continue with the drug, it became time for my wife to give me her view. That morning she had just experienced some dizziness, her voice became even more slurred and other forms of the drug's side effects also showed up. It was as if she was given a reminder to think wisely, as she was about to make her decision to do the right thing. For my wife, that right thing was to take a leap of faith. We were sitting in the living room. Her pills were usually kept over the refrigerator in the kitchen. Between the kitchen and the living room there was no door. Depending on your position in the living room, you could virtually see almost everything in the kitchen. She got up and walked to the refrigerator and took out the pills. She said to me, "Daddy, this is not my battle. God didn't save me to suffer from this drug's side effects. I am no longer going to take it; God will continue to fight for me." As she spoke those powerful words, she was on her way to the trashcan to throw the box of pills away. I ran after her and asked her to give me the pills. She gave me the box of pills and I put it in my pocket with the intention of hiding it, just in case she might need it later. I still wasn't faithful enough to agree with her. I was terribly shaken by her action and felt that I would fail in my role if I didn't help her make the right decision.

At this moment, it was difficult for me to tell whether or not my wife's decision was well founded, considering all the searches we had done. But on the other hand, her action was not a surprise to me. I had known my wife to play a major role in our home when it comes to the things of God. As I noted in the previous chapters, her mindset suggests that God's blessings are never followed by sorrows. But after those many difficult days of hospitalization, I found it hard to believe that she could still continue to hold onto her faith. So, whether her leap of faith was in the positive direction or not, I was yet to find out. As it turned out, she proved me wrong again. For the next few weeks I would learn once again what it means to take a leap of faith. Instead of taking her medication, she chose to exercise 30 minutes each day and avoided those foods she was asked not to eat. The symptoms and side effects recurred temporarily. As time went by, they disappeared without her taking the medication.

As I see it, with every major hitch we came across, there was a miracle from God. In the face of all the warnings we were given and read about Coumadin, I was surprised to see my wife cross yet another stage in her struggle against blood clots after she had abruptly stopped taking the drug. As I look back and realize the many obstacles that stood in our way but became crushed by the power of God, it was about time to count our blessings, naming them one by one.

I could not agree more with a friend who once said, "Any medication that comes from God has no side effect." Although my wife began to exercise regularly and ate the right types of food she was told to eat, I believe these were only supplemental to the Lord's unseen medication that has guided her through to this day. She made a choice to put the Lord in control of her health problem and so He took charge of it and gladly healed her.

In reality, the words of faith my wife used that morning as she was walking towards the box of pills, "This is not my battle," if rearranged, could be read this way: "The battle belongs to the Lord." *The Battle Belongs to the Lord* is a song by Jamie Owens-Collins. Coincidentally, the lyrics of this song fit well with my wife's misfortune:

> *"In heavenly armor, we'll enter the land,*
> *the battle belongs to the Lord;*
> *No weapon that's fashioned against us will stand,*
> *the battle belongs to the Lord;*
> *And we sing glory, honor, power and strength to the Lord,*
> *We sing glory, honor, power and strength to the Lord.*

When the power of darkness comes in like a flood,
the battle belongs to the Lord;
He's raised up a standard, the power of His blood,
the battle belongs to the Lord;
And we sing glory, honor, power and strength to the Lord,
We sing glory, honor, power and strength to the Lord.

When your enemy presses in hard, do not fear,
the battle belongs to the Lord;
Take courage, my friend, your redemption is near,
the battle belongs to the Lord.
And we sing glory, honor, power and strength to the Lord,
We sing glory, honor, power and strength to the Lord."

©1984 Fairhill Music, Inc
Used by permission. International Copyright Secured.

In this song, one can hear and feel a message from the Lord that speaks to the heart of my wife's situation. The song speaks of strength and courage; it is about a battle that we do not see with our naked eye—a journey of suffering and hardship we had not expected. The words of the chorus, "the battle belongs to the Lord," are words to calm the storming sea. In Psalm 121:5-8, the scripture teaches the following: *"The Lord is thy keeper; the Lord is thy shade upon thy right hand. The sun shall not smite thee by day, nor the moon by night. The Lord shall preserve thee from all evils, He shall preserve thy soul. The Lord shall preserve thy going out and thy coming in from this time forth, and even for evermore."*

My wife's leap of faith demonstrated by her decision that day was nothing short of God's protection and her trust in the Lord. She knew it would only take the power of God to appease our fear and bring our search for more information on the effect of Coumadin to an end. The information we had found through our Internet searches was still useful, but instead of going through it by ourselves to prevent an onslaught from another blood clot, she entrusted every part of it to the Lord.

It was in February of 2008 when we made this decision to stop the Coumadin and it was about three months into our darkest moments. At that time we were four months away from fulfilling our promise to pay a visit to Africa to see her parents, especially her mom, Mama Karambiri. This trip would be the first time in five years since Daniella had seen her mom. It was important to go and see her, not only because of the many years she had been away from her, but also and most importantly, for Mama Karambiri to see her first grandchild, Baby John. Her mom couldn't wait to see the baby.

Every now and then she would call and tell her daughter to take the phone to the baby to have a chat with him. But the baby was only three months old. It was impossible to have him talk. Mama Karambiri would insist to hear the baby's voice by some other means, but we couldn't devise any means to fulfill her wish. I remember my wife told me one day when I got home from work that Mom had called at about 6 P.M. Eastern Time and said she wanted to hear the baby cry when my wife was giving him a bath. Mom got the time difference mixed up. There is about a five hours difference between us. For example, when it is 8 A.M. here in the US, it is 1 P.M. in Burkina Faso, West Africa. It was also difficult to work out a timing to suit her schedule due to appointments and other routines in connection with the baby's care and hospital visits. The reality was that the baby was not colicky; he wouldn't cry when you gave him a bath. From the time he was born, the nurses at the hospital had noticed that he was a peaceful baby and mostly quiet, unless he was hungry. We could also not keep him hungry just to make him cry; I guess that would be an abuse and Mom would not like that either. It was disappointing to John's grandmother.

Mama Karambiri's reaction and excitement about the baby was not a shock. Looking back, it was long overdue. We all paid a price for that long awaited day. So, apart from the normal behavior of first-time grandparents, we learned that friends who teased her that her daughter was barren had mocked my wife's mother. In fact, prior to her pregnancy, I had suggested that my wife should visit her parents back home, but she refused to do so. When asked why not, she told me, "Mom said I shouldn't go if I do not have a baby." In a typical African setting such a situation is not uncommon. So it was easy for my mother-in-law to quickly overlook her daughter's recovery and to celebrate the birth of the grandchild she had longed to have. She was tired of being scoffed at and of being put to shame. But despite all of Mom's anxiousness to see the baby, there was only one way to satisfy her. That way was to cut short our waiting period and leave for Africa as soon as possible.

But there was a reason why we could not do so. In most cases, it is customary to travel overseas with a baby, especially to Africa, after the baby is at least six months old. At this age the baby would have had the necessary vaccinations. During our consultation with his doctor, we were reminded of the same protocol. There was also another reason for waiting. My wife was still in her recovery period. It was important to follow every prescribed step ahead of us to avoid the unexpected. As would be expected, these impediments kept us from going and Mom would be left with no other option but to wait.

As time went by, Mom was able to hear the baby cry on the phone. Sometimes he would make some noises, and of course she couldn't make any sense of them. She would express a sense of fulfillment that she had heard from her grandson. Mom was able to hear the voice of the baby because she called at least three times a day to keep up with the time difference. It was an unrelenting and dedicated effort to give her what she wanted and at the time it was much needed.

By the middle of February, precisely on the 15th, Mom sent her older daughter, my wife's sister, Sarah Karambiri, to visit us. Mom does not like to travel, especially by plane. I am sure that was the third reason that prevented her from seeing her grandchild at that time. I am convinced that she would have been here for the delivery of her grandchild to take care of him from day one and to be the one to tell the story of his birth to the rest of the people back home. Sending Sarah Karambiri, she wanted to be sure we got the help we needed after the many weeks of our troubles. Sarah Karambiri was here with us in the US for a month. She helped us greatly during my wife's recovery at home. When she left, we still had about three months before our planned trip back home to Africa.

If the Lord were to reveal what the future holds before it actually arrives, words like doubt, unexpected, surprise, shock and others of the same ilk would have had no place in the dictionary. That is why He is such a mighty and wonderful God whom we serve. Perhaps, if He let us know what lies ahead of us, so many horrible things would happen beforehand and the world would be in total disarray. Placing the veil over tomorrow tells us more about His wisdom and greatness. As you will learn later, we would be confronted by another surprise—a surprise that would change our lives forever and be the reason why understanding the truest meaning of life would remain uncertain for years to come. It was a tragedy that awaited us behind a dark cloud.

CHAPTER 7
THE PASSING OF MAMA KARAMBIRI (MY WIFE'S MOM)

> *"To everything there is a season and time for every purpose under heaven; a time to be born, and a time to die. A time to plant, and a time to pluck what was planted. A time to weep, and a time to laugh; a time to mourn, a time to dance."*
>
> *Ecclesiastics 3:1-2:4*

INDEED, THERE IS TIME TO BE BORN AND A TIME TO DIE. No human can ignore this reality, regardless of race, economic, sociopolitical status, and because such reality has no age discrimination, it lies before us unavoidably. It is said, "The world is a stage where we have come to do our part; when our time is over, we leave." The good thing about leaving the world stage is that when you are a Christian, the Bible tells us that we have a place, a home to go to, to live perpetually. *"Let not your heart be troubled; ye believe in God, believe also in me. In my father's house, are many mansions; if it were not so, I would have told you"* (John 14:1-2). Death itself is part of the plan for salvation to Christians. One of the ways we can see the Lord is through death. That is why when death comes, the Bible teaches us to rejoice.

Our happiness was short-lived after my wife recuperated. The plans to visit our baby's grandparents back in Burkina Faso, Africa, became even more disorganized. When Daniella's sister, Sarah arrived in the US on the 16th of February, their mother continued her regular calls, two to three times every day, to keep in touch with us and her grandson.

Two weeks later, while Sarah was still here, Mom complained of fatigue during one of their telephone conversations. She also said that she had visited her doctor and had the necessary tests and procedures done and was awaiting the results. Just about that same time, I also spoke with Mom. Our conversation ended in a song that I couldn't wait to sing to someone for the joy of my wife's recovery. That was my first time talking to Mom since my wife was discharged from the rehabilitation center. It was a song of praise to the Lord for my wife's recovery. It is a song I always sing when I experience the glory of God. I sometimes change some of the lyrics to suit the situation. For my wife's situation, this was the way I put it:

> *I am so glad that Jesus loves me;*
> *He restores my wife from death,*
> *He refused for my son to be motherless,*
> *He spelled victory over preeclampsia,*
> *He spelled victory over blood clots,*
> *Despite my sinful nature,*
> *I am so glad that Jesus loves me.*

Because of the changes I had made, it was not a song I expected Mom to sing along with me. All she did was to mumble the words to go with the tempo. We didn't sing for long; it took about two to three minutes. At the end, she prayed and blessed my family.

Three days before Sarah left, she and my wife called home to speak to Mom, but they were told she was tired and was taking a rest. They didn't get to speak to her. March 7th was their dad's birthday. They called to wish him happy birthday and asked to speak to Mom, but again, Dad told them Mom was taking a rest.

There were no suspicious signs, as Sarah puts it. "I have known my mom to be someone who doesn't like to go to ceremonies, as she would soon become tired." The communication and information about Mom continued this way, until it was time for Sarah to go back home to Africa. Her visit ended on March 8th, 2008, and her trip was planned for the 9th. She left according to plan. Normally, it takes two days to get to Burkina Faso with a transit in Paris, France. We learned later that there was some rough weather on her way back home between Paris and Ouagadougou, the capital of Burkina Faso. The plane had encountered similar weather when she arrived in the US on February 16th. It had to make an emergency landing in Nashville, Tennessee while the weather stabilized before flying back to Atlanta, Georgia where she was transiting to the Tri-city Airport in Tennessee. Sarah finally made her way to Ouagadougou safely after having encountered rough weather over French territory.

If signs that were seen to be meaningful in ancient times meant anything to us today, the inclement weather Sarah experienced twice while coming and going would have given her an insight as to what lay ahead, as she made her way back home. For example, when the flood was over, the Lord showed Noah a sign that became a covenant between Him and mankind. He said, *"I set my rainbow in the cloud, and it shall be for the sign of covenant between me and the earth. It shall be when I bring a cloud over the earth, that the rainbow shall be seen in the cloud. And, I will remember my covenant which is between me and you and every living creature of all flesh; the waters shall never again become a flood to destroy all flesh"* (Gen. 9:13-15).

To Sarah, and the rest of us, the signs meant nothing, even when she told us the story about how difficult it was in the air on her way to the US. I remember telling her, "It would have been better for me to have picked you up from Nashville, since you were already in Tennessee." We all laughed and joked about it and let it go. If there were anything more to do, it would have been a few words of prayer and thanksgiving to God for her safe trip to us. After all, she had made it and we could not have asked for anything more. Little did we know that we actually needed more than a few words of prayer. If we had given importance to the meaning of the signs and taken seriously the unusual things that were happening around us on a daily basis—the rough weather or the rainbow—it would have given us food for thought when Sarah told us the story.

When Sarah got home from the airport in Ouagadougou, the news she heard was a bombshell. She was told that Mom was dead. March 10th, 2008 was the very day she landed in Ouagadougou, Burkina Faso. Imagine the shock, imagine the agony and place yourselves in Sarah's shoes. What would the world around you at that moment look like? What would be your initial response? And if there were any tears at all, how many would roll down your cheeks? If life meant anything, it has to be nothing compared to death. I was told that Sarah's initial response was none other than passing out. She was speechless for hours. The news was beyond her comprehension; even to this day, the question, "I wonder what exactly happened to Mom?" remains on her lips and mind.

But that was how Sarah got the news of Mom's death. If there had been any recollections of the inclement weather she had experienced on the trip, reality would have begun to sink in that something unusual was about to take place. Thankfully, that is one way the Lord conceals information from us to prevent devastation from happening. Back in the US, we were expecting a call from Sarah on her arrival in Ouagadougou. As you can imagine, it was not Sarah telling us about her safe arrival; it would be someone else on the following day in a voice that would be breaking up with emotion.

March 10th was the second day since Sarah had arrived in Ouagadougou. We knew she had reached home and thought that it was not necessary to call immediately since she would need some rest from the long journey. If we needed to call Sarah it would have been between 8 A.M. and 3 P.M. local time because of the five hours' difference between us. On that day, it was already 2:30 P.M. and at 3 P.M. I had to go to work. So we postponed our call until the next day. Before going to work, I packed my lunch into my lunch box and left. I had no reason to hurry on my way to work. The journey was as short as three miles. I left at 2:30 P.M. just to take my time on my way.

The first 30 minutes on the job is an overlap period. During that time the shift changes and information is given to the incoming staff on what is needed as a priority and sometimes there would be a brief review of the paperwork. This helps to put both teams on the same page. After I had completed these normal routines usually associated with the shift changeover, as supervisor I had to organize my report that was due in a few days. It was about 3:45 P.M. and I was still in the middle of my paperwork when my cell phone rang. I picked it up and saw that it was a private call. I was about to turn the cell phone off, thinking it was a call from some business promoters, but I quickly realized that I could always say no if I had no interest in whatever they were promoting. So I turned the phone on and answered it. From the other end I heard the voice of my father-in-law. It was then about 4 P.M. Eastern Time. With five hours' difference, it was about 9 P.M. to him. Although he had called me at work before, it was never as late as this. I honestly didn't expect a call from him at that time, especially at 9 P.M. local time. I also thought that if it had anything to do with Sarah's arrival, he wouldn't be calling that late.

"Hello," I answered. He asked, "Where are you?" "I am at work," I replied. He sounded unhappy, but I had no idea what this was about. There was nothing within my wildest imagination that could possibly tell me what his call was about and why he was sounding so upset. I became a little concerned. The next thing he said was, "If you are standing, take a seat; what I am about to tell you is important." With this, it became evident that something must have gone wrong, but what it really was still did not occur to me. Before I told him that I was now seated, I intentionally took about 45 seconds, quickly trying to figure out what he was going to tell me.

We had not had any discussion of this kind before; in those few seconds I was trying to prepare myself mentally and also emotionally. I finally told him I was now seated and ready for what he had to tell me. As with Sarah, my share of the bombshell was about to be dropped on me. He said, without any beating around the bush, "Mom has passed." The news didn't penetrate quickly. Even though he wasn't going to tell me any elaborate tales, I still had no reason to immediately believe what he was saying. For one fact, it was less than a week earlier when Mom and I had joyously sung praises to the Lord. She sounded normal and I was happy to talk to her. Secondly, I had not heard anything about Mom being seriously sick since we last spoke. If this were true, what then could possibly have killed her? I began to think like Sarah. Not being too sure what was being said, I probed for more information in a rather dramatic way. "What?" My father-in-law then repeated the message. He finally said, "Get someone to go with you before you tell your wife." With this suggestion, there was no time and no need to ask for further details. I was mute for a while.

This news abruptly changed my entire afternoon, leaving me with several pictures on my mind. I could see my wife going back to the hospital for readmission; I could see myself finding ways and means to get a baby-sitter, and I could see a rerun of the entire period of her hospitalization. I could also see myself falling deeply into depression, having almost completed a marathon of a near-death-experience with my wife's sudden fall due to blood clots. When I dropped the phone after the call, it took me another hour to begin planning for my next step. I summoned my on-call staff member and explained the situation. As God would have it she was able to send another staff member to relieve me so that I could go home and take care of the situation.

I was relieved to go home, but my usual three miles' journey became even longer than ever. The question I kept asking myself as I drove home was, *What am I going to tell my wife and how am I going to say it?* But I realized that no matter how I would say it, no amount of eloquence would be enough to convince her to immediately accept the reality. Apart from finding ways to present the case, I was also still in a state of shock myself. And worst of all, my wife was still frail, fresh from the hospital. I was not convinced that I should even tell her.

As I got closer to the house, I was reminded that I needed someone to be with me before anything was said. The only person I could think of was Pastor Bernard Zougouri. He had been with me all the way during my wife's days of hospitalization. I made a stop at a gas station nearby, about a mile from my home, to call him. By then, he had already received the news from Africa. He assured me he would be with me the next morning. I finally got home, but could not look my wife in the face. As if sensing that something was up, she did not ask me why I was back home from work so early. The only thing she told me was, "I have not talked to Mom for about a week; I need to talk to her tomorrow morning." Tears immediately gathered in my eyes. I quickly hastened away into our bedroom. If only she knew what had happened, we would be having a different discussion and not talking about a phone call to Mom.

I wasn't too sure how soon Pastor Zougouri was going to get to us in the morning, as he had promised. During that waiting period, I didn't know what to do. I couldn't sit around my wife for even five minutes. I was always finding something to do away from her. I think it is fair to say that I was terribly battered by the news. At the same time, because her family was so well known in their country, I was afraid that someone would call to sympathize with her without knowing that the news was still being kept from her. In that difficult situation, it was only God I depended on to help me through.

At about 8 P.M., my wife's uncle, Lasana Karambiri called from

Pennsylvania. He had already received the news as well and was calling to let me know he was on his way. I told him my predicament and he encouraged me to keep holding on, even though he was about a nine hours' drive away. As I hung around the house, pondering and worried, I was in constant communication with Pastor Bernard Zougouri. He advised me to find a way to get my wife's cell phone away from her. But that too was difficult. I had to have a reason for doing so; otherwise, my cover would be blown. So, each time I received a call from Pastor Bernard Zougouri, I had to walk out to answer the call. Such suspicious behavior kept going on and on. As God would have it, the night deepened so quickly that the possibility of receiving a call waned. What remained was the guilt caused by my knowing what had happened to my wife's mother and sleeping on the same bed without telling her. I spent the night without a wink of sleep. My imagination ran wild on just about anything unpleasant. My family had been at the center of attention in the last four months. The unavoidable questions were, *what next? How am I going to get out of this situation and why is it happening to me?* That night was a period of internal weeping with episodes of rhetorical self-questioning. Being badly inflamed by the situation, I was even more worried about the outcome in few hours when Pastor Zougouri would arrive to reveal the news to my wife.

At about 9 A.M., Pastor Zougouri and his wife Isabelle arrived, but because my wife's uncle was also on his way, I told him to wait. I thought that the greater the number of people present, the better it would be for me. So we had to wait for a while. My wife's uncle arrived later. Just before she was going to be told, something happened. A boy who happens to be a church member of her dad's church back in Africa was here in the US attending college. He was apparently browsing from one website to another and he ran into the news about my wife's mom's death. The information was already everywhere. He picked up the phone and called my wife to let her know. Closely following the conversation and noticing how my wife's countenance was changing, Pastor Zougouri intercepted the discussion and magically turned it into something different.

We were all very cautious because of her condition, but as much as we tried to keep the news away from her, it became even more difficult to do so. A few hours later, they took her into the kitchen to give her the news. There were six persons around her in the kitchen as we prepared to tell her. It was about noon after she had had something to eat for lunch. My wife's response to the news would not be a surprise. As a human, her behavior was consistent with what we tend to do when such unbelievably appalling things happen.

Even as I write this story, remembering what my wife's reaction was when she was told, saddens me to this day. "Oh, God, why, why?" She went on to cry, "Mom will never get to see her grandson." As you can imagine, this was not where signs of bravery or strength come in; regardless of one's gender, age, a clergyman or a counselor—everyone, including myself, could not hold back our tears. The emotional outburst expressed on everyone's face in the kitchen at that moment reflected so many passions, which confirmed that the event was not ordinary. *How could a person recovering from a death experience pass through this again? How could she not weep and mourn for someone she needed and expected to be with in just a few months? Who was there to strengthen her through motherly love that she had missed for five unbroken years? And how and why did God decide to put these events so close together?* My wife's reaction was just the beginning of something more serious to come. The rest of the story and trauma would set in when everyone returned to their respective homes. I would then be the only one to contend with it—in the morning, in the afternoon and in the middle of the night.

It wasn't too long before Pastor Zougouri and my wife's uncle went back to their respective homes. We were still in the second week of March. Our previous plans to take the baby home to Grandma fell apart. At the same time, our home became a constant reminder of all the horrible events of the previous four months. If you had looked at the wall in our living room with pictures of my wife's parents taken in the good days, and considered what had taken place, it would have reminded you that things had greatly changed forever. The obvious thing to do was to get away for a while to allow time to heal the newly created wound. But the only possible place we thought of going was Africa to see my wife's brothers, sister, and Dad. With about three months to go, every night was a difficult experience.

Sometimes in the middle of the night, my wife would be asleep and suddenly she would shout, "Mama, bye, bye, Mama, bye, bye." When I awoke from sleep frightened, thinking there was an intrusion in the house, I would see my wife's hands in the air, facing the wall, while she was saying goodbye to her mom. I would grab her hands, saying, "D.Q., D.Q., please stop!" The situation would go on for the next 30 to 45 seconds before she would realize that she was having a dream. For the rest of the night we would be awake, staring at each other in awe of what was going on with our family. As for my wife, she would be in tears all night long.

On other nights, she would be heard speaking her local language while asleep: "Mama, umbi-tala, Mama umbi-tala." When translated into English, it means "Mama, I am coming." It was as if the images of readmission to the hospital I had visualized from the onset when her dad told me the news were becoming a reality. Every day the situation developed into a new but devastating experience. Understanding how sensitive his daughter is, her dad called three times a day from Africa to speak to her and calm her down. Even that only helped for a while.

The real problem this created for me was that every one of her friends and family members that came around during her hospitalization had left.

It was not likely for them to come back and be with her, knowing their busy schedules in America. That meant, there would be no one to stay with her to encourage her, as they used to do. The good news was that they called her on a regular basis to check up on her. I had only asked for two days to be off work because I knew that in about three months I would be asking for three weeks to take my wife and baby to Africa. After my two days of vacation, my wife was left alone with the baby at home. Thankfully, a lot of our community friends were still around to see her from time to time when I was away at work.

Although I was afraid that the situation might greatly depress my wife, I was wrong. It was not God's intention to let my wife drift into depression or to be readmitted to the hospital or to rehab. The agony, sense of loss and sorrow we felt was normal. Anyone in our position would agree that from a human perspective, death is always unfair, untimely and disliked, even if it takes away those who are 100 years old or older. When death appears, not even the contemplation of God's words, that life is like a vapor, can give us consolation, especially if it happens to one of our own. We still become apprehensive regarding the true meaning of life as defined with the clarity of scripture. This is all natural. Until the day of His second coming, a time when we will be given the opportunity to see those departed faithful loved ones again, our behavior towards death will continue to taint our faith in the Lord and continue to make us nervous of its meaning.

I have learned through this experience that when the Lord appears to be far away from us in times of crisis, it becomes difficult to deal with the situation with maturity. In all this, because of the cold hands of death and the chills and pains it brings upon family members, more often than not we forget that as Christians, part of the plan for our salvation is through death. One of the ways we get to see the Lord is through death. It is inescapable.

I have also learned that my wife's behavior demonstrated her intense love. In our seven years of marriage, if I have learned nothing else from her, it has been love and compassion. A few months before her pregnancy in 2007, one of my cousins' wife gave birth to a baby who passed away a day after delivery, even before she was discharged from hospital. We went to the hospital to comfort the parents and to take them home to be with us for some time. Before we left the doctor asked if we wanted to hold the baby for the last time. The mom and the dad nodded no in response, perhaps to avoid further pain. On my part, for reasons unknown, I also turned down the offer. The only person left in the group was my wife. She stepped forward and said to the doctor, "Give me the baby." She told the baby, "Baby, come, let me hold you. I know, if you go to heaven, you will tell the Lord that Aunty Daniella was the last person to touch you." I do not know about the others, but my wife's response exposed my own weaknesses and unfounded fear. The doctor stood amazed; perhaps that was the first time he had ever seen anyone do that.

Her behavior would be repeated several months later after her mom's death. Fast forward—as we waited for our baby to be old enough to travel to Africa three months from the day we got the news of Mom's death, there were many times when my wife would be influenced by her feelings for her mom. Every moment of solitude she had was a moment of weeping. Morning, noon or bedtime were all opportunities for an emotional release with tears. The most distressing moment for me came one day when I got home from Wal-Mart after purchasing a few items for the house. She was sitting in the bedroom with the baby about five feet away from her, asleep. She was on the phone with tears rolling down her cheeks. My initial suspicion was that she was talking with her dad. After about three minutes, she was still on the phone, but saying nothing. I began to wonder why she was not talking. I asked, "D.Q., who is on the phone with you?" She said, "I just called Mom's cell phone to listen to her voice." My wife's reaction seemed to demonstrate yet again her sense of melancholy. She had not accepted the reality that her mom was dead.

Time became the first healer of our wounds from the perilous days: the surge of blood clots, subsequent clinical death and Mom's passing. But there was still a need to develop proper coping skills and a strategy to deal with the ever-present reality. Friends, family and church members helped enormously to keep us confident again. That was good; the timely intervention of these people would never be forgotten.

But nothing is more comforting than the word of God. We turned to the Bible for our source of strength and comfort. The scripture says, *"We are hard pressed on every side, yet not crushed; we are perplexed, but not in despair; persecuted, but not forsaken; struck down, but not destroyed"* (2 Corinthians 4: 8-9). Once we became much more aware of our situation and were given the courage from this passage and many others, we launched into our family creed: *"Ask, and it will be given to you; seek, and you will find; knock, and it will be opened to you. For everyone who asks, receives, and he who seeks, finds, and to him who knocks, it will be opened"* (Matthew 7:7-8).

This was just the beginning of the healing process. As is often said, "The counting of numbers always begins with the number one." We needed to strengthen ourselves first to be able to deal with others in a more mature way, as our trip to Africa was fast approaching. As usual, each day we went to bed and got up in the morning with prayers, knowing that all we were seeking from God at the moment was strength and comfort to be able to overcome the situation. The reality was that Mom was gone; there was no scripture to tell us in our devotional or meditative time that she was coming back the following day. To confront this reality, we chose another way to seek comfort and strength. It is to be more practical in making peace with reality.

One must be able not to ignore the live evidence and accept the prevailing conditions. We must learn to leave tomorrow with its own problems alone, since we have no clue what it may bring. Looking to the Lord, the provider of strength, peace, love and comfort, was our strength. Also, because we believe that there is hope, even in death, when life on earth ends, we must hold firm in our faith and look to the unchanging hands of the Lord. That promise to any Christian is an assurance that helps seal our faith in God and is helpful to squarely confront reality.

As for Mom, it was not for us to pass judgment as to how she lived her life on earth before her departure. In hindsight, we believe that her going home to the Lord was a victory. It was a victory in that from what we saw and knew about her life on earth, we were convinced that she was with the Lord. Of the many options we all have as to how to live, she chose to live a simple Christian life. The scripture says, *"He who believes and is baptized shall be saved."* Mom did not only accomplish that, but each day, in many ways, she fought for her salvation with fear and trembling. We also believe that it is not our perfection that takes us to heaven but that it is by His grace. We believe Mom led a life that demonstrated a remorseful and repentant spirit. As humans, it is tempting to be blind to the truth, but a repentant spirit makes all the difference. That too was exemplary in Mom's life. In our minds, and to those who knew her and what she stood for, her life on earth was not in vain but a victory over temptation, trials and tribulation, suffering and a whole host of things that can easily take our attention away from serving the Lord.

It is often said, "Only time is capable of understanding how great love is." This statement feeds into the intense love my wife has for her mom. Despite the encouragement from the word of God through the scriptures and others, to this day my wife continues to wish for many things. "I wish Mom was still alive so that I could do this or do that with her...," "I am missing Mom...," "Mom and I had a plan for my second child. She said she was going to be with me when I gave birth." The stories of Mom never end, especially when a day like her birthday, Christmas or New Year's approaches—a renewed spirit of love burns in her. With time passing, the sorrow has vanished, but time has never been able to take away her love for her mom. She now perceives it from a different point of view: "Mom is in heaven and her life is worth emulating." In her marriage she vows she will continue to be faithful to me, just as her mom had been faithful to her dad.

In writing this book, I could not leave out the insight of the man who, apart from God, knew Mom better than I did or her children did. Since Mom became his wife at age 26, and they had raised four children, they spent a lot of time together, under diverse circumstances as Christians in a country densely populated with Muslims and adherents to other traditional beliefs. Until her death, they had been married for over 30 years. It was a marriage that began when he completed his studies in Toulouse, France in the early 1970s earning an M.A. in Economics and continued while he served his country, Burkina Faso, from 1975 to 1989 in several managerial capacities. Standing 6 feet 3 inches, Pastor Dr. Karambiri is known to be bold, straightforward, and a man with a great sense of organization in his work for the Lord. I asked Pastor Dr. Karambiri to tell me a little about Mom's departure and her influence on him as a husband. I have written down his comments as they were given to me. I did not add nor subtract anything. He wrote this in outline format for clarity. Here is what he had to say:

"Mum's departure for heaven can be described as follows:
Preparatory stage
2007 was the preparatory year during which Mum started to feel that she was going to leave.

Difficult relationships she had with some people improved markedly.

She used to talk a lot about our future without taking herself into account within this future.

She was watchful regarding her spiritual life by repenting continuously as if she did not want to be surprised by her departure.

Week two of departure
This week was full of enigmatic words and prophetic signs. Mum was tired in her body, but her spirit was still alert.

Three days prior to her leaving, she was projected into eternity and during these days she kept talking to me about a trip she was to undertake. She called people to give them advice, to bless them and to encourage them to work faithfully with me.

On the opening of the Rhema Media Center-television studio (i.e. on Friday, March 7, 2008), she attended the ceremony despite the fact that she was tired. Guests and many brethren of the church who also attended the ceremony noticed that her face was glowing with a particular glory.

On Sunday, i.e. March 9, 2008, after the service, she called me and told me about the trip. I went back home quickly where I found her surrounded by the children who were sitting with her and she was blessing them. I sat near her on the bed and after we talked for a while, she turned onto her left side, raised her right hand and

started to worship the Lord. It is at this moment that she
went into a coma on the same Sunday afternoon.

On Monday, March 10, 2008 she went to meet her
Lord in total peace at 10:10 P.M. Glory be to God!

The impact of mum on my life:
She was a modest, humble woman who refused to
live beyond her means. She contented herself with what
her husband gave her.

Concerning our relationship, she was faithful, very
loyal and transparent.

She proved to be an unfailing support and a great
advocate of her husband vis-à-vis outsiders.

She respected her husband and prayed a lot for her
family.

These qualities she kept, improved over the 33
years of our marriage, may inspire her children and
particularly her two daughters with their respective
families.

During the last three months of her life, she
communicated these qualities to many young couples
that came to seek advice with her. Today, she is with the
Lord, and she is happy, totally fulfilled and in peace."

It was certainly a daunting time for my father-in-law, as it was for me,
spending several days by his daughter's bedside and a few months later losing
his wife. As he has been a man of God for many years, I thought there
was something to learn from him from these experiences. I asked him the
following question: "From a Christian perspective, being a preacher, what
did these crises teach you about faith and belief, especially considering your
direct involvement?" Here is what he wrote:

"In Psalm 11:3, Psalmist David declares, *'if the
foundations be destroyed, what can the righteous do?'*
In Hebrews 10:18, God states, *'My righteous one will live
by faith.'*

When Christians are faced with any kind of crisis (family, physical,
economic, and so forth), God expects them to trust Him. Our trust in the
Lord shows up and develops itself only in situations where we learn to know
Him through His faithfulness, love and confidence.

While I was facing my daughter's death (she was declared dead clinically),
I kept my faith in the goodness of the Lord and the accomplishment of Christ

on the Cross. My feelings and emotions were strongly weakened. However, in the deepest part of my spirit I decided to trust the love of Jesus Christ for my daughter, my son-in-law and my grandson.

Despite the negative and hopeless statements by some physicians and nurses, I kept waiting for the power of the resurrection of God who created everything and for whom medicine limitations are not a problem. The 18 days I spent at my daughter's bedside and with my son-in-law were days of faith and spiritual struggle. Crisis reveals to Christians the type of faith they have: a faith crippled by circumstances, fear, and other people's opinion and words or a faith like a mustard seed, which takes root into the word of God, struggles, resists, hopes, perseveres and receives by the grace of God.

Sarah was barren; Abraham's body was already worn-out. Despite these scientific facts, both of them hoped against hope, and their faith did not fail. They believed in God's faithfulness, in a God who listens when the poor call for Him and turn to Him when they are in distress. Let us remember that the one who promised is faithful."

The account of my father-in-law was inspiring. He was willing to share his personal experiences with me. And despite the difficulties, the way he managed to remain strong in his faith was another key to understanding him. As I noted above, it was difficult for me to recognize his emotional state throughout that time. From the way he conducted himself, I thought he embodied a strong lesson about faith.

Indeed, there are a lot of lessons to learn. One of them is, "Maturity. It has more to do with what types of experiences you have had and what you have learned from them and less to do with how many birthdays you have celebrated." As God would have it, my wife came out of this with a high degree of maturity about life. Thankfully to the Lord, the woman whom doctors thought would be living a meaningless existence after all of the difficulties with her health and despite the trauma that followed immediately with her mom's death, she went back to school, with plans of studying to become a Business Manager. The first few weeks in college (National College), she experienced some difficulties writing and comprehending her lessons.

At one point she told me she was giving up the whole school idea. I encouraged her and we prayed about it. Before the end of the semester, things changed for the better. She finished with a grade point average (GPA) of 3.65, majoring in Business Management.

CHAPTER 8
BENEVOLENCE;
THE CHURCHES' RESPONSE TO OUR CRISIS

"Now all who believed were together, and had all things in common, and sold their possessions and goods, and divided them among all, as anyone had need. So continuing daily with one accord in the temple, and breaking bread from house to house, they ate their food with gladness and simplicity of heart."

Acts 2:44-46

"And let us not grow weary while doing good, for in due season we shall reap if we do not lose heart. Therefore as we have the opportunity, let us do good to all, especially to those who are of the household of faith."

Galatians 6:9-10

I BELIEVE WHOLEHEARTEDLY THAT Christianity is not only a religion but also a way of life. A keen look at the passages above gives one the idea of the kind of life Christians ought to live. To a social scientist, a sociologist, for example, a way of life is simply a culture—how people live. So, the choices Christians make as to how they lead their lives say more about what sets them apart from the rest of the human race and other cultures in the world.

When I became a Christian 22 years ago, I quickly learned that I was in a totally different environment. People I met in the church referred to one another as brothers and sisters. In addition to that, brethren met in fellowship to join hands together around a bowl of food. There were a lot of fun times; we made one another happy and stayed together in oneness of spirit. What I also noticed was that the preacher had no prejudices in terms of the choice of people that he spoke with. He shared with everyone and was even willing to accommodate jokes from the little ones at all times.

But that was not all. I also realized that brethren were habitually engaged in praying for one another's problems: financial, social/marital, health and even for the nation… In addition to the prayers they offered on each other's behalf, those who were financially able did not hesitate to help others in need. There were a lot of commonalities among brethren that made me feel at that time and even now that Christians have a unique way of life that sets them apart from other people.

In general, the simplicity of Christian life could not be better explained than with the example of the support I experienced when my wife collapsed on December 8th, 2007. This support made me question why it took me so long to become a Christian when part of what you know and learn is empathy and sympathy from people about your spiritual and physical wellbeing.

In those youthful days in the church, I decided to read the scriptures to have a better understanding of the practices. I soon realized it was not by chance that brethren were engaged in their way of life. They were following the example of their leader, Jesus Christ. A follower must do the will of the leader. If Jesus is the head of the church, He determines the direction of the people. For example, when Jesus met Peter who was trying to fish for his daily bread but could not catch any fish, He showed Peter how compassionate He was. After He performed His miracle and Peter caught a lot of fish, He commanded Peter, *"Now you will be a fisher of men."* He also healed the cripples, He made the blind see, He fed many hungry people with five loaves of bread and He raised the dead. Jesus met the physical needs of these people and then provided the spiritual lessons for their salvation as well. Jesus' examples fit squarely into the culture I ran into when I entered that environment 22 years ago. That experience was like being a newborn babe in that tiny West African Country of Liberia where I started. It was the same in Ghana where I lived for eight years and mingled with other brethren. It didn't change in Burkina Faso where I met my wife and it is also the same here in the United States.

Like me, somewhere in the West African State of Burkina Faso, the woman who would become my wife also had her own experience of "the Christian way of life" under the guidance of her father and mother. That was why it was such a delightful experience when we met. We share the same beliefs: a sense of benevolence and struggle to embody the Lord's teachings on the subject of compassion.

In the church, racial, gender, national and class lines are blurred. Whether you are black or white, poor or rich, woman or man, American or African, we are brethren because we believe our true citizenship is in heaven, where our true identity is determined. Regardless of one's education, we are still our brothers' keepers. Whenever the need to help arises, we are of one accord. The vice president of the hospital where my wife was admitted, John Melton, happens to be a brother in the church. A man of that status, whose socio-economic standing could not be compared with mine, took time off from his very busy schedule to visit with us almost on a daily basis. As you can imagine, his presence in my wife's ward at the hospital was encouraging to nurses, doctors and other care providers. I was told later how he encouraged the doctors to do more to provide services to my wife. Most often it is only within the churches' environment that you have people with such a simple lifestyle.

The very day my wife collapsed, it was a brother who spread the word. In a matter of minutes, Brother Timothy Hall, the minister was there to comfort me, even before any member of my family knew. The church met our needs both physically and emotionally as they arose. Brethren were moved by the same spirit that had moved those in the early church to go from house to house with the simplicity of heart. The elders, the preacher and several members visited my wife each day throughout her stay at the hospital. I didn't have to worry about my rent and bills; I didn't have to worry about food. Everything was taken care of by the church. But that wasn't all the help I received from them at the hospital. Whenever I ran into some misunderstanding with the nurses, brethren were immediately there to take care of the situation.

These benefits were just the physical aspects of the assistance my wife and I received. There was also the spiritual intervention. As I pointed out, Brother Tim, my preacher, was the first to appear on the scene when the incident took place. He was also the first to offer a few words of prayer. He didn't stop there. When he left the hospital, the information about my wife's deplorable health condition was circulated among brethren. That information was sent on the church's website and emails were also sent out to every member, asking for special prayers.

Not satisfied by the help received so far, the church assigned a brother and an elder to me, making sure that all of our needs were adequately communicated to the church for extra assistance. They wanted to do just about anything I asked of them. I realized that their presence was not only about meeting the needs that they were aware of; at times I needed someone to encourage me. A brother, in particular brother Kent, would come and tell my wife, "You need to get up and come to church this Sunday." He knew she was non-responsive, but he was making every effort to give me some encouragement. He would joke and make me smile, just to add a little life to my dull and lifeless condition. The presence of the brethren gave me the confidence I needed to work through those difficult times. At times, when I would leave the hospital to settle some other issues, I would see sisters from the church on their way to the hospital with fruits, get-well gift cards and other necessary items for my wife and our many visitors. The fact that they also thought about our visitors speaks volumes. Not only that, it was also in many ways a fulfillment of the scripture, *"Let us do good to all."* On the whole, the influx of church members always made my day, as I sat close to my wife pondering our plight. It gave me a sense of belonging, a feeling that I was not alone.

The church in Johnson City, Tennessee was only the forerunner. There was another group based in New York that my wife and I had never heard of before. A few days after her fall due to blood clots, the word spread quickly across the nation and beyond. One of our friends in New York heard the story. Instead of coming down to see us, she thought that the best way was to take our case to the Lord in prayers. She was a member of a prayer group based in New York. I was told that they fasted and prayed for days. At the end of each day she would call to check in on my wife. Every time she called me, there were always encouraging words, "The Lord is in control, do not worry," she would say.

Also, in Ghana, West Africa, there was another minister of the gospel, Minister John Korsinah. We had known him prior to my wife's pregnancy; he was one of those people who had prayed with us for a child. When he heard the story, he called me and said, "I am on my way to the mountains now." In the mountains, he found a place of solitude to fast and pray for as long as he felt he needed to. It took him a number of days, close to a week, before he called me back to check in on my wife. When he called, all he wanted to hear was that Daniella was okay. For him, like the rest of the people who prayed, the answer to the prayers was a restoration of life to its fullness. Like others, to this day Minister John continues to wish God's blessings upon us so that we may have more children.

I would describe it as "a binge of prayer season." Everyone we knew added his or her voice to the chorus of prayers from everywhere. But it got even more intense with the involvement of the group from Burkina Faso where my wife's dad preaches to an audience of over a thousand people in one sitting and ten thousand people in all of the congregations he has established. I was told that my wife's dad was in church when the news reached him. He subsequently informed the members and went home. On the church's compound there is another building, three stories high. It is called the prayer tower. In that building, the prayer warriors took turns day in and day out, 24/7, praying and fasting for my family, my wife in particular. She grew up in that church; friends, family members and everybody else knew her. Praying for her was like praying for your biological daughter, sister, aunt etc. The love she commands in that church among members was evident on our visit after her recovery when we gave our testimonies to the church gathering. There were tears, praises to the Lord and happiness for her recovery. See picture in Appendix B.

PART II
A REFLECTION ON THE PAST;
FURTHER FINDINGS

CHAPTER 1
THE IMPACT OF BARRENNESS

"And her adversary also provoked her sore, for to make her fret, because the Lord had shut up her womb. And as he did so year by year, when she went up to the house of the Lord, so she provoked her, therefore she wept, and did not eat."

1 Samuel 1:6-7

"Thus hath the Lord dealt with me in the days wherein He looked on me to take away my reproach among men."

Luke 1:25

LIKE HANNAH MENTIONED IN THE BOOK of 1st Samuel and Elizabeth in the book of Luke, my wife wept for so many days and nights through five long years, hoping to become pregnant, until 2007, when the Lord finally answered her prayers for a child. As a result, Baby John, whom many now call a miracle child, was born. Five years was a long time to wait, to pray and to be labeled a barren woman. In many cultures around the world for a woman to be called barren is a stigma that lowers the woman's viability and renders her fruitless and unproductive. Many think this derision is an ancient practice, but it still continues today. As you will discover as you read further, it was this stigma that slowly made its way into my wife's life and changed it forever. The stigma that she could not have a child, a label she had never dreamed of having and didn't even believe fitted her description, caused tension that grew by the day and turned into stress. As a result, her blood pressure became uncontrollable. Those who were in the business of censuring her and calling her barren were people she saw every day and people her parents knew very well. It was a situation that became permanent, and without a pregnancy, this situation would continue. Most importantly, for people with African backgrounds, the idea that a married woman is barren puts the entire marriage in jeopardy and the parents of the woman are constantly looked down upon.

The truth is, my wife and I love children. After we married and my wife's first pregnancy ended in miscarriage, our love for children did not cease. In our community we became babysitters for our friends. We treated their children with the love we would have given our own. But as it happened, that was not enough to silence the critics. Their comments kept coming again and again in different ways. Somewhere along the line, I inoculated myself against further embarrassment. I disregarded their taunts and pretended that I was not a target. I realized that for many men, it is easy to get away with that kind of attitude since it is almost always assumed that men do not have infertility problems. My wife, on the other hand, could not pretend. She wanted children of her own, but beyond that, news reaching us all the time from her mother back home in Africa confirmed that she was taking a lot of heat from her friends as well. My wife always tried to fulfill her dreams and promises she had made to me after our wedding: "Daddy, I am the mother of your children, the children you will always be proud to have." As time went on and failing to fulfill this promise, she felt she could not take no for an answer.

With this continuous unacceptable behavior from people, it became necessary to question this age-old tradition that marriage is only meant for childbearing, a tradition that doesn't seem to go away, but continues to pervade people's attitudes in the twenty-first century. I began to address it with the question, *What if we don't have a child at all in this marriage? What if we adopted a child, if we cannot have one of our own?* I went on asking "What if, what if…"

These questions opened a Pandora's box of answers related to other people's experiences and the decisions they had come up with to help me make sense of it all.

CHILD BEARING AND SOCIAL PRESSURE

THE PRESSURE EXPERIENCED BY MY WIFE and myself regarding child bearing was understandable, given our African background. Perhaps one may conclude that in most African societies marriage is intended solely for reproductive reasons. To put this within a larger context, the Hebrews' Bible, which serves as bedrock of world history, concurs with the fact that one of the major reasons for the creation of man and woman was to replenish the earth. For example, in the Book of Genesis, chapter 1: 26-28, the Bible says this: *"Then God said, let us make man in our own image, according to our likeness; let them have dominion over the fish of the sea, over the birds of the air, and over the cattle, over all the earth and over every creeping thing that creeps on earth. So God created man in his own image; in the image of God he created him; male and female, He created them. Then God blessed them, and God said to them, be fruitful and multiply; fill the earth, and subdue it; have dominion over the fish of the sea, over the birds of the air, and over every living thing that moves on the earth."*

Regarding the African context, Paul Kishindo notes in his article, "Family Planning and the Malawian Male" that barrenness in a woman is a valid reason for divorce in Malawi. Not only has the man the right to a divorce in the wake of barrenness, he points out, but he also has the right to demand traditional payment—cattle (*lobola* in local Malawian language) from the bride's family if his wife fails to bear children. By the same token, in Ghana it is believed that a family is the foundation for assigning reproductive, economic and non-economic roles to individuals.

There are other aspects of child bearing to take into consideration regarding cultural differences. For example, the issue of nature versus nurture in problems of differential fertility is another concern. Paul Landis (1959) notes that there is much evidence that a differential birth rate still exists in the United States and that by and large most children are born to those least able to give adequate nurture. On the other hand, he points out, there is also some evidence that the differential birth rate may be unfavorable from the standpoint of eugenics. Those with the least ability, he adds, may still be having more than their share of births; those with the most ability, fewer than their share. Landis argues that this situation is vital in a democratic society, which believes in individualism and stresses the right of every child to be born into conditions which offer him or her the greatest prospects for nurture and development. Mary Ann Lamanna and Agnes Riedmann (2000), on the other hand, note that variations in birthrate among couples reflect values and attitudes about having children. They point out that in traditional societies, couples don't decide to have children.

To put it succinctly, they add, children just arrive and preferring not to have any at all is unthinkable. But addressing the issue of social pressure, Lamanna and Riedmann observe that married people who don't want to have children face problems. Although these pressures are lesser than in the past, they note, our society still has a pro-natal bias—having children is taken for granted, whereas not having children must be justified. Some of the strongest pressures, they point out, come from the couples' parents who often have difficulties accepting and respecting their children's choices about whether to have children, let alone their decision about when and how to have them.

Another important aspect is the cost of child rearing. Richard T. Schaefer and Robert P. Lamm (1992) cite a 1980-census survey that found six percent of married women between the ages of 18 and 34 did not expect to give birth in their lifetimes. The same survey found another 11 percent of widowed and divorced women who felt the same way. A similar survey by the U.S. Department of Agriculture, conducted in 1990, found that the average upper middle-class family would spend $265,249 to feed, clothe and shelter a child from birth to age 22. This estimate excludes college tuition.

My research concerning external pressure on couples to have children, especially women, confirms that there are huge similarities across cultural lines. People in the third world, including most African societies, are not the only people to still traditionally expect every married couple to become parents. In the West some still maintain this traditional view among both married couples and their parents. A typical example is the story of Lynnell Michells entitled, "Why We Don't Want Children." This story appeared in the book, "Current Issues in Marriages." She writes, "Married nearly five years and no children yet? Don't be discouraged, my dear, my sister and her husband tried for nine years before she got pregnant. Just keep trying and you will succeed."

This brief paragraph was a comment made by Lynnell's mother-in-law's old friend. This type of comment, according to Lynnell, has the potential to annoy some women. But she notes, "I was amused." She points out that, rather than laugh and offend my mother-in-law's old friend, I merely nodded knowingly. She adds, "Catching my husband's eye, I saw that he too was working to keep from grinning."

What Lynnell observes in this encounter is the fact that people are quick to lay judgment on others, even if the facts are not available. She calls this an "automatic assumption." She points out that never once had she and her husband planned to have a child since they had been married. She notes, "I have been on birth control pills." Lynnell was not a barren woman; her decision not to have a child was a matter of timing and all the important considerations that are part and parcel of child-bearing and child-caring had been taken into account.

Lynnell's experience was like that of my wife. When we first got married, it was not difficult for her to become pregnant—she became pregnant in the first month of our marriage. That pregnancy lasted for only two months, after which she had a miscarriage. We did little to take care of that problem after the miscarriage. Later, after my wife saw several gynecologists, they all came to one conclusion—that she would have no problems with future pregnancies if we intended to have children. Such information is not usually shared with the public; it was our family personal issue that we wanted to keep private. Those who were not informed about these issues—the miscarriage, the doctor's visits and the report that my wife could still become pregnant if we wanted to have children—became the most virulent critics that mounted so much pressure due to her assumed barrenness. So, while they might have been right, based on the cultural belief that marriage is all about having children, the automatic assumption noted by Lynnell is a major problem that tends to cause unnecessary interference in other people's private affairs. Understanding the couple's real problem (if there is one) and contributing to their cause, if required, might be a more positive way to approach the situation.

As a teenager, I had witnessed first hand what it meant to be married without a child. I had the opportunity to live with my aunt who had been married for several years without having a child. For a while it seemed that she was comfortable in the marriage and there was no mention of a divorce, at least not at the time when I lived with her. But what I didn't see in that marriage, that was apparent in most other marriages, was the presence of the husband in the home. We lived in a small village of about 50 people. For the two months that I was there, I never saw my aunt's husband spend a day at home. He was virtually absent all the time. Whether or not this was an agreement between them, it was a strange situation. The reason for his absence in the home became clear later when I returned to my parents in our village. My aunt came back and reported to my dad that the man had divorced her on grounds of barrenness.

At the time, as a child, I did not understand the how and why of the man's absence because growing up, my mom and dad were always at home caring for us. But, as I pondered over my aunt's return to our village, the obvious conclusion I could reach as a child was that the man hated my aunt. I was only a child; if I had understood the cultural implications then, I would have had a different view. Little did I know that the barrenness of a woman could be construed as a kind of curse, a sin, a condemnation, failure, embarrassment or even a tragedy that has the potential to expel a woman from her marriage. What I didn't understand then, made sense during the brief period my wife and I experienced being ostracized. It made sense because the traditional African approach to marriage is generally to expect every couple to have children. I was told that my aunt had been married for over ten years to the man. My guess was that she was extremely lucky to be in such a relationship for that long. Looking back on my aunt's plight, I can clearly see that she was in a living hell. It was a piece of that hell that my wife and I experienced in the first five years of our marriage.

From this experience it became clear that barrenness was not the only drawback in marriages that I observed in the 17 years of my adult life on the continent of Africa before my arrival here in the United States. Nine of the 17 years were spent in Liberia, the country of my birth and eight of those years in Ghana, another West African country. According to my observation, it was uncommon for a couple to make the decision not to have a child and to then happily live among relatives without any problems. It was not a common practice for a couple to adopt a child to settle the issue of barrenness in a marriage. Usually, a child found in the home of a childless couple is either a maidservant or a child of a relative who was sent there for education purposes. The implication here is that the problem of barrenness cannot be compromised and virtually, there are no options available to the couple that would satisfy either parents—the rules seem to be written in black and white.

On the other hand, it seems that with the passage of time, the western culture, for example, in the United States, has overcome most traditional beliefs about having children and there is help available to women or couples in making their decision whether or not to have children. In the last ten years since my arrival in the United States, I have seen a stark change in people's ideas about adoption and child bearing. History tells us that since the baby boom era in America, most Americans have developed a different attitude towards child bearing. European-Americans seem to have fewer children these days, while most minority groups, for example, Hispanics, African and Asian Americans tend to embrace the idea of multiple births. In his book, "Current Issues in Marriage and the Family," J. Gipson Wells (1988) notes that the American family of the 1970s are now entering an unprecedented era of change and transition with a massive reappraisal of the family and its functioning; divorce rates are on the increase, marriage is redefined and childbearing is becoming the sole decision of the couple, without parental involvement." Wells indicates that with increased knowledge and effectiveness of contraceptives and the spread in their use, especially among the middle class, the idea of limiting family size began to be acceptable and later on reached the point of being almost mandatory.

Also, Schaefer (2003) views childbearing as "cultural universals." Cultural universals, according to him, are general practices found in every culture, which represent the line of connection that brings, if not all, most cultures around the world together concerning the expectation of childbearing among married women. Despite the similarity that may exist, Schaefer notes that cultural universals differ from one society to another and they also may change dramatically over time within a society. He points out that each generation, and each year for that matter, most human cultures change and expand through the processes of innovation and diffusion.

Mingled with this wing of change, as Wells puts it, is the women's liberation movement which has caused more and more young couples to begin questioning themselves about whether or not they want to have children. There are several reasons for this decline in the birth rate, but as one of my former professors of sociology puts it, "Americans are educated." She was not the only married woman I knew without a child at that university; there were several others, all of whom were happily married without children. There were also other professors in the university with adopted children who were happily married while leading their professional lives.

Cara Swan, a member of Childfree Organization of America, a group that promotes the cause of freedom of choice in childbearing, says this: "I think we childfree should consider creating our own worldwide day of recognition. I can just imagine the antagonism this would garner from the childed, but it could be a way to spread our message: Not everyone has to reproduce, happiness can be found without having children." Cara is not the only promoter of childlessness and I think that advocating for freedom of choice for women as to issues of childbearing—for those who think it is impossible, given their medical conditions or other factors, or for those who are still waiting—must be given its due support.

The question of whether or not to have children depends on many things. Leslie Lafayette, founder of Childfree Network, points out that there are several different reasons why people joined the organization. Some women have infertility problems, others choose not to have children at all, and some never found the right mate. She also says, "Infertility is not a disease. No one ever died from it. It's unfortunate, but there are so many children to adopt."

PERSPECTIVES ON MARRIAGES

WHEN MY WIFE AND I BEGAN TO FACE pressure from home and abroad (Africa) from relatives, friends and others, all of whom were Africans, the situation created not only confusion, but led us to question our decision that had brought us together. *Did we make the right choice to be married; should we have had a fertility test before our wedding; whose problem really was it?* These intriguing reassessments of our relationship tainted our determination to stay happy and focus on our future goals. It made us take a closer look at our relationship as others saw it—a relationship that in their view was bound to fail and it was only a question of time.

Many questions come to mind: *What is marriage and what are the conditions for its stability? What does it really take to make a marriage successful? Is the question of having children a tradition that every couple must fulfill?* These questions were a stone throw away from the much-needed answers to our predicament. Dealing with these questions requires further discussion that would bring into focus what marriage is from different perspectives—egalitarian versus traditional. Here I will attempt to discuss briefly the two types of marriages—egalitarian and traditional—and their impact on those involved, like us.

Egalitarian marriage, according to Bale Norman, is a marriage without any authority structure. Such marriages, he notes, are also known as partnerships and peer marriages. In an egalitarian marriage, he adds, everything operates on an equal path. For example, tasks and responsibilities are equally shared, there is no such thing as a woman's work or a man's work, co-parenting is the order of the day in child-rearing for those with children, and intimacy or love is a major concern to both partners.

Traditional marriage, on the other hand, extends beyond the spectrum of an egalitarian marriage. It involves the couple, the families on both sides and the community. Defining it within an African context, traditional marriage, according to Cormac Burke, places the emphasis on children. Speaking of marriage in this sense, Burke is cautious to address the topic in specific terms but chooses to generalize his concept of the definition of marriage as it might vary from one African nation to another. Africa, according to him, does not have one kind of culture, but the similarities and approaches to marriage could be generalized. He notes that because the emphasis in marriage is placed on children, the birth of a child marks the consummation of the marriage, thereby keeping the marriage from dissolution. Considering the high value Africans place on children in marriages, Burke notes that a woman who does not give her husband a child in marriage is considered a failure to him and the society at large.

In these brief definitions of the different types of marriages (egalitarian and traditional), two things are worth noting: first, love as a central focus in egalitarian marriage and second, children as a condition for a successful marriage within the traditional arrangement.

MARRIAGE AND LOVE

THE WORD LOVE HAS A LOT OF DIFFERENT meanings. It could be used to describe feelings about an object or the emotions and affection a couple has for one another. It is my intention in this book to focus on the family type of love as espoused in an egalitarian marriage with the application of a scriptural viewpoint. To begin with, love, according to *dictionary.com*, is defined as a feeling of warm personal attachment or deep affection, as for a parent, child, or friend; a profoundly tender, passionate affection for another person. Biblically, it is impossible to have a discussion on the topic of love without considering John 3:16, which teaches that, *"For God so loved the world that He gave His only begotten son, that whosoever believe in Him, shall not perish but have everlasting live."* John 3:16 is not directly applicable to the type of love mentioned here. However, there is one lesson we can draw from it, that makes the quotation useful.

The Bible teaching in John 3:16 describes the lesson of sacrifice. Sacrifice in this context is a requirement for any type of love. For example, Ephesians

5:28-33 says, *"Husbands love your wife in the same way you love your own body and yourself"* (Ephesians 5:25), *"Husbands love your wife as Christ loved the Church"* (1 Corinthians 7:3-5), *"Your body belongs to your wife"* (1 Peter 3:7), *"Be considerate as you live with your wife"* (Proverbs 5:20), *"Do not be captivated by other women"* (Matthew 19:5), *"Be one flesh in every way"* and in Hebrews 13:4, *"Marriage is honorable among all, and the bed undefiled; but fornicators and adulterers God will judge."*

Here, it is quite clear to note that every aspect of love as seen in these scriptures requires some level of sacrifice to maintain a relationship. One has to make a radical decision to turn away from things once loved and devote one's time to one's wife or husband to fulfill what is required to meet the standards of love. From the egalitarian standpoint mentioned, it makes sense to accept the premise that marriage is based on love. After all, without love no marriage can possibly prevail.

MARRIAGE AND CHILDREN

THE IMPORTANCE OF CHILDREN CANNOT be emphasized enough. In most cases, when one thinks of marriage, the idea of having children forms part of the planning process. When a couple plans for the future, children are considered. A society that places its hope on the family, indirectly addresses the issue of future leaders. A Chinese proverb rightly puts it this way, "One generation plants the trees, another gets the shade." In a similar vein, Mother Teresa once said, "If you want to work for world peace, go home and love your families." These quotes speak volumes. Relevant to this subject is the argument that there would be no need to work for world peace in the first place if the future was not everyone's concern in terms of the next generation. The future as suggested in this quote has more to do with children or the youth. One era in American history that confirms this attitude is the time of the baby boom, which was brought about by the understanding that children represent the essence of continuity of life into the future.

From the Christian perspective, children are an essential part of the Kingdom of God. In Mark 10:13-16, the Bible teaches the following: *"Then they brought the little children to Him, that He might touch them; but the disciples rebuked those who brought them. But when Jesus saw it, He was greatly displeased and said to them, let the children come to me and do not forbid them, for such is the Kingdom of God. Assuredly I say to you, who ever does not receive the kingdom of God as a little child, will by no means enter it."* Still expressing his ardent love for the little children, Jesus said in Matthew 18:6, *"But whoever causes one of these little ones who believe in me to sin, it would be better for him if a milestone were hung around his neck and he were drawn in the depth of the sea."* Christ also said in Mark 9:37, *"Whoever receives one of these little children in my name receives me; and whoever receives me, receives not me but Him who sent me."*

As we can see, the importance of children as demonstrated here couldn't be overstated. They represent the future of the nation and the Kingdom of God. So, when those within a traditional marriage argue that child bearing is a primary focus in a marriage, it makes sense to accept such an argument on the basis of the evidence provided above.

BARREN WOMEN ARE CHILDREN OF GOD

Our story is just one of a million other stories out there. I suspect that we may not be the only ones to voice our frustration caused by people's response to suspicions of barrenness. As mentioned above, some people are already beginning to speak out against the traditional social norms regarding the issue. We did not choose to become a statistic. The fact that we have gone through this struggle, and saw how devastating it was, is the reason why I have taken interest in writing on the subject of barrenness. First, given the argument on both sides of the debate, I am convinced that having children is a decision that needs to be made by a married couple alone. I also believe that no marriage can survive without the presence of love. In essence, children and love are the major components of a marriage.

This said, I am especially worried about the plight of barren women—women who wish to have children but cannot; women who would be prepared to take care of their children if given the chance to have them but are limited by barrenness; women who through no choice of their own became barren and have to find ways to remedy the situation and live continuously in suppression, in reproach, in ridicule and torment from friends, relatives, co-workers and in some cases from their own husbands. As an individual with an African background, a place where the traditional marriage is still a predominant presence, I know first hand what it means for a woman to be barren in a marriage. Not only will she be stigmatized, but the parents as well as her siblings are also ridiculed. I remember what my wife had gone through during the five years when we waited patiently—the intense pressure from her friends, relatives and others is material for stories we will continue to tell our children.

Also, stories about my aunt and millions of other women who ended up in divorce due to barrenness are worth telling. The cultural pressure exerted upon many of these women today puts them at high risk, to the point of committing suicide. They feel rejected by society; they feel life has no meaning without a child and they feel the institution of marriage does not belong to them. And because I have witnessed this twice, first with my aunt and then my wife, I saw it fit to add my voice to the chorus of those who hunger for peace to live their life freely as women and as humans made in the image of God, just as those with a multitude of children do.

As I pointed out earlier, the primary goal of most married people is to have children. But children are not the only bedrock of marriage; love is equally important. In the event that children are not forthcoming, a divorce or the stigmatization of the woman should not be the solution. For Christians, there is no account in the Bible that says a man should divorce his wife on grounds of barrenness. In a Christian home where the problem of barrenness is an issue, the couple should be the ones to bring to life the good examples from the Biblical stories on the subject of barrenness.

It seems to me, when it comes to the issue of barrenness, it is a generally accepted idea that men usually do not have a problem. This idea subscribes to patriarchal traditions where men are the voices in the community. To me, it is only designed to put further pressure on the women. Such a concept about infertility is a fallacy. Men as well as women are both at risk of infertility. All we need is to be empathetic with one another to have a happy marriage, whether there are children or not. In the West where modernity is making great strides in replacing traditional lifestyles, there are still some elements of rivalry between men and women on the issue of barrenness. In Africa and Asia, it is an ongoing phenomenon. It is said that in India, for example, "a barren woman has a high risk of public rebuff in a way that she is viewed as someone with an incomplete life; if she works for money, many wonder why she works if there would be no one to inherit her savings when she is dead." Each woman, with either a temporary or permanent infertility problem, is vilified in this way.

There were days when my wife would come home very quiet and sad. On a day like this she may have been told something related to child bearing. One day she went out on a picnic with a group of friends; among them were two of my younger cousins' wives, both of whom were mothers. One of the girls scornfully said, "We are the fruitful wives in this family"—meaning the Quewea family. That sarcasm was clear and well understood. My wife knew she was automatically being isolated from the rest of them as an "unproductive" wife of the family. That mockery was just one of the many she received.

Long after her delivery, people began to confess what their secret plans had been. According to one of them, they were finding means to take my wife away from the marriage. But that plot would have been dead on arrival. It wouldn't have met my approval. I love my wife regardless of her situation. To me, being barren is not a crime; neither is it a sin in the sight of God.

Given the horrific treatment women receive at the hands of pro-natal individuals, which I think will continue unabated, I am of the view that to counter it will require a concerted effort by a concerned group of people like myself or anyone who may have experienced similar problems and who knows how difficult it is to help challenge this annoying behavior towards our wives, sisters, mothers, aunts, friends, nieces, cousins and other acquaintances. To allow the marriages of these people to end in ruin, to tolerate their being scolded on a daily basis by people whose interference is nothing but negative, is unacceptable. Marriage is a relationship that brings a man and woman together; if child bearing is a concern, the couple must be allowed to deal with the problem by themselves without external interference. They may choose to see a doctor and if that doesn't work out, the last resort is to seek divine intervention. God is just and righteous and will answer their prayers, according to His will just as He did for my wife and myself. It becomes more difficult to deal with the problem of infertility if the husband seems not to understand the woman's plight at the hands of others.

In the case of my wife, I deserve no praises from her or anyone for the level of patience I exhibited during our five years of waiting; it is all God's doing. While it was true that we wanted children, all I did was to play my part as a loving husband, even in the face of our dwindling hope. When outsiders were pressuring my wife, I thought she needed me to fill in the gap, expecting me to be a friend, a brother, a father, an uncle and a husband, to help stabilize the situation. Above all, we all need God in those difficult moments to answer our prayers. This was one thing we learned through this tortuous time.

Perhaps, like any other couple seeking help in a crisis, we listened a lot to the voices of the very people who overstated the actual magnitude of our problem. As a result, we lost control over our privacy and our family's decision-making ability. We thought that by so doing we were on the right path, seeking a better solution to our problems. But that wasn't the case and in the end we created weapons against ourselves. This experience taught us to say no sometimes, even to our significant others. We have realized that it is impossible to please everyone; it is rather more liberating to take control of your decisions and the choices you make when it comes to the most crucial issues of your life. Had we done this, perhaps we would have saved ourselves the tension we experienced. However, after the dust had settled, we realized that the criticisms, belittlement and other forms of slur we experienced did not only hurt us but they also helped strengthen our love and faith in God. This was a realization of the scripture. In James 1:3-6, the Bible teaches that the testing of your faith produces patience.

Another thing we learned during these years was that despite the difficult times, we never once chose divorce as a last resort, but rather loving one another became our primary focus, since the goal of having children was receding away from us. There are many people out there like us, whose marriages are undergoing similar struggles and they may be on the verge of a divorce, or there may have been some fighting concerning irrelevant issues. They may have had the feeling that life is no longer meaningful and the only option they now perceive is either suicide or homicide to end it all. I must say to those people that if the whole world around you has rejected you because of your barren situation, God has not; there is still a chance. Your day, like ours, is coming and life will change forever. As a couple, we can now consider those events as arrows that point to the past. They have become stories to inspire others when they are told. Using this experience, we are well placed to counsel those involved in a similar situation. If we can do it, you can as well. All it requires is a little bit of resilience, patience and faith in God.

Giving up would be a weakness, but developing a strong sense of commitment to one another provides a determination to live through your crisis. It is not about being overly optimistic or being in stark denial of evil as it exists in life, but recognizing your problems, and knowing that to every crisis there is a solution is a good way to overcome our difficulties. So keep hoping and believing and, above all, trust that God will see you through.

BARREN WOMEN AND GOD'S MIRACLE

GOD DEMONSTRATED HIS POWER WITHIN the lives of many women in the Bible. Almost all of these women have become household names in our Christian community today. The work of God in their lives shows not only His faithfulness in answering prayers but it also tells how faithful the women were and how loving their husbands were as well. Sarah, the wife of Abraham, for example, was barren for many years; she was old enough for the prospects of child bearing to no longer be considered, until a word came from God that she was going to have a child. Not taking it seriously, she laughed, but within God's timing she conceived and gave birth to Isaac (Genesis 16:21). Also, the wife of Isaac, Rebekah was barren for 20 years, then the Lord came into their lives and she gave birth to Esau and Jacob (Genesis 25:21). Rachel was another on the long list of barren women. She was married to Jacob for several years without having a child. Rachel cried many times, blaming Jacob; Jacob would reply angrily, saying, *"I am not God to withhold the fruit of your womb."* But God, knowing their problem, wiped away Rachel's tears; she conceived and gave birth to Joseph and Benjamin (Genesis 30:1).

The name of Samson's mother is not mentioned in the Bible, but the scriptures note that she was barren for a long time before she had a son (Judges 13). Elkanah married Hannah—one of the barren women of the Bible. She pleaded with God to give her a son and God blessed her with Samuel who became the greatest and last judge of Israel (1 Samuel 1). Elizabeth and her husband Zachariah also prayed incessantly for a child; Zachariah was so old that they had given up hope, but with God, all things are possible. God blessed them with a child who became known as John the Baptist, the greatest prophet and forerunner who prepared the way for Jesus Christ (Luke 1).

Psalm 113:9, *"He grants the barren a home like a joyful mother of children."* Praise the Lord! It is a burden when women are faced with infertility, especially if the husbands or parents are not sympathetic to the situation. But, as the scripture points out, all is not over; a joyful day might still appear ahead. We are also reminded that the solutions to our problems can be found if we humble ourselves before the Lord and simply ask Him. In John 16:24, the Lord says: *"Until now you have asked nothing in my name. Ask, and you will receive, that your joy may be full"*; in Mark 11:24 Jesus also says, *"Therefore, I say to you, whatever things you ask when you pray, believe that you receive them, and you will have them."*

While planning for our wedding in 2002, I had the time to intensively look through all of my favorite scriptures to select the one best suited for the invitation card. The idea behind my intensive search for this scripture was not about being Biblical or to portray myself as a staunch Christian, but sometimes some things stick with people. On a day like a wedding, a very important part of a couple's life, there is always something to remember. One of those mementos could be a quote from scripture, which usually commands people's attention. So, a well-chosen quote from scripture could be one that the couple would dwell upon in the future and serve as a basis for the family philosophy.

Above all else, the scripture chosen should be able to bring God into the marriage in some way, in good or bad times. I picked Matthew 7:7-10. It says: *"Ask, and it will be given to you; seek, and you will find; knock, and it will be opened to you. For everyone who asks receives, and he who seeks, finds, and to him who knocks it will be opened. What man is there among you who, if his son asks for bread will give him a stone, or if he asks for fish will give him a serpent?"* Copies of this passage were not left at the wedding grounds when the ceremony was over; they have since been used as a guide within our marriage, in all of our problems, especially during the five years of waiting for a child. The same passage could work for any family hoping for children or anything else from God. Do your part, and the miracle of God will set your feet upon the rock and your future will be established.

MORE ON PREECLAMPSIA

MANY MONTHS LATER, AFTER WE WENT through these experiences, I began to research my wife's disorder (preeclampsia). See below from the research.

Preeclampsia Foundation (PF) defines preeclampsia as a disorder that occurs only during pregnancy and the postpartum period and affects both the mother and the unborn baby. It is a progressive condition characterized by high blood pressure and the presence of proteins in the urine. The symptoms of preeclampsia, according to the foundation, include hypertension, swelling or edema, proteinuria, sudden weight gains and changes in vision. The report further notes that preeclampsia is a disorder that occurs after 20 weeks of gestation (in the late second or third trimesters, or middle to late pregnancy). The Preeclampsia Foundation is a non-profit organization dedicated to funding research, raising public awareness and providing support and education for those whose lives have been touched by preeclampsia and other hypertensive disorders of pregnancy.

There have been thousands of others like my wife who were unaware of this disorder and had been affected by it. Many thanks to the foundation and its good work in an attempt to create the awareness needed to bring the presence of this deadly disorder to public notice. Globally, the report notes, preeclampsia and other hypertensive disorders of pregnancy are a leading cause of maternal and infant illness and death. The estimated number of deaths is 76,000 maternal and 500,000 infant deaths annually.

The curiosity that led me to this website to peruse further information about this disorder has injected more fear into me, as a result of what I have read and learned, which is more than what my wife's doctor had explained to me. Other websites, such as The World Health Organization (WHO, 2005) confirm the Preeclampsia Foundation's findings. It puts the preeclampsia number of deaths at 12 percent, running fifth from the bottom of the list of deadly forms of silent killers, such as obstructed labor and other direct causes, which are both at eight percent of all maternal and infant deaths. Unsafe abortion stands at 13 percent, infection—15 percent, indirect causes—20 percent and severe bleeding (hemorrhage) at the top of the list with 25 percent.

On its website the foundation cites over 950 stories of survival, following a case of preeclampsia. Each story I read brought chills to my heart. Here is how the foundation summarizes the women's stories: "Because this condition is transitory in nature, women become members of a silent club, experiencing a crisis and in some cases a traumatic event, without emotional or physical preparation or the support of women who have been there before. All too often we are told we should be grateful to be alive, to be healthy, to have a baby, to have had our baby for just a little while."

In these stories most women survived without their babies or the babies survived without their mothers. The experience usually leaves an indelible mark on the surviving parents or babies that remains forever. As I searched from Website to Website and from books to books, looking up preeclampsia, nothing I read about it was encouraging; it was just one of those silent killers that many people have never heard about sufficiently.

The statistics regarding preeclampsia indicate that the disorder can be more dangerous than anyone had imagined. A survey conducted by the Preeclampsia Foundation indicates that over half of all pregnant women are not informed about its signs and symptoms, and that as a life threatening condition, it complicates one in twelve pregnancies. The results from the survey also point out that the incident of infant death is twice as great for women who give birth prematurely and are not properly educated by their healthcare providers. Also, in a survey of more than 1,300 women who had given birth, approximately one third reported a premature birth (under 36 weeks' gestation for this survey). The report notes that of the premature babies, 18 percent were either stillborn or died within the first year from birth-related complications, as compared to one percent of babies carried to full term.

The foundation's statistics further states that in 2002, approximately five to eight percent of pregnancies were affected by preeclampsia. This means that more than 6.6 million women worldwide suffered from the disease that year. Preeclampsia causes 15 percent of premature births in industrialized countries and it is the number one reason doctors decide to deliver a baby prematurely. In the United States, the report indicates that preeclampsia is responsible for approximately 18 percent of all maternal deaths. If undetected, the report notes, preeclampsia can lead to eclampsia, which is one of the top five causes of maternal and infant illness and death, causing an estimated 13 percent of all maternal deaths worldwide or literally a maternal death every 12 minutes.

CHAPTER 2
THE LESSONS LEARNED

"Blessed is the man that endureth temptation: for when he is tried, he shall receive the crown of life, which the Lord had promised that love Him. Let no man say when he is tempted, I am tempted of God; for God cannot be tempted with evil, neither tempted He any man."

James 1:12-13

NO MATTER HOW COLORFUL WORDS may be, in describing an incident that took place in the past, it is still difficult to get your message across with the necessary precision. Perhaps movies or photographs are the only sources that can do a much better job in conveying the totality of the true nature of an event. Throughout this book, I have tried my best to present my family ordeal to you, the reader, in the best way possible. In this section, "The Lessons Learned," I present a recap of the entire story.

Prior to my wife's pregnancy, I knew that one of the disorders associated with pregnancy was pregnancy-induced hypertension (PIH). That is when the woman's blood pressure goes up during pregnancy. Most doctors agree that such a condition is common to most women. Whether PIH leads to preeclampsia or not is still a question under some debate within the medical community. The consensus from many studies is that a woman's risk of preeclampsia is higher if she has had a history of high blood pressure prior to her pregnancy. Other than this, things like high-risk pregnancy and preeclampsia were not part of my vocabulary. I didn't know about them. Perhaps this was due to my lack of interest in medical science.

I was forced to quickly pay attention to this subject when reality began to set in from my wife's diagnosis. I became a student over night and learned the hard way. But the hardest lesson, as you may know by now, became the blood clot that sent shock waves across the hospital the moment it happened.

In my extra research, and the preceding records, I have provided more details to address the genesis of how it all happened. It started with the stigma that my wife was a barren woman. The intensity of that led to stress and the stress of being stigmatized led to high blood pressure. The blood pressure was poorly controlled due to the continuous presence of those who exerted unnecessary pressure upon her. They were our friends, our relatives and friends of my mother-in-law. Because the high blood pressure was poorly controlled, even before her pregnancy, it became even more difficult to deal with it when she was pregnant. It was at this time that her pregnancy developed into a high-risk condition, which subsequently developed into preeclampsia. Preeclampsia necessitated a C-section delivery and a day later, blood clots brought about the worst experience yet.

Each step of the way, the miracle of God guided us across another bridge, another bridge and another bridge. My family and I will remain forever thankful to the Lord. As I pondered over this each day following the various episodes, two potentially important lessons came to mind. I have explored these lessons in general terms in the previous chapters but it is important to be specific here, as I conclude this writing. The first is the cultural effect of child bearing. One of the reasons why the pressure was so intense on my wife for being barren was because of our cultural background. In most African cultures, a woman's role in the marriage is to bring forth children. If she fails, she is considered unproductive and cursed. The question then is, what would have happened if those family members, friends and friends of my in-laws were people who believed in our privacy and didn't care whether or not we had children? Would my wife have been under such stress as to develop high blood pressure and everything that followed later?

The second lesson is the obvious question anyone in our position would ask. Lord, why me? Couldn't you have spared me from this trauma? These questions are familiar. Job and even the children of Israel asked the same questions. These were the same questions I asked and when my wife regained consciousness, she also asked the very same questions. You could also imagine all the barren women of the Bible asking God in the same manner. When Job asked these questions, God answered him in a way he had never expected. It was a miracle. When Sarah and the other barren women of the Bible thought they could no longer have children and had given up every hope, God finally made the difference. That too was a miracle. When Daniel was placed in the den of lions and everyone thought he would be devoured in a second and when Shadrack Meshad and Abenego were put in the lake of fire, a fourth man was there with them to guide them through to safety. All of these were God's miracles.

I had always believed in the adage that says, "Behind every dark cloud there is a silver lining." One of the differences between those who are Christians and other people in the world is the ability to understand the will of the Lord. In times of trouble or when we are beset by difficulties, the questions, When will it be over? How soon am I going to get out of this? will always tend to blur our view of Him. This expectation will lead us to asking, "Is He a father who answers prayers?"

The examples above underscore God's way of demonstrating His miracle to men. He comes in to rescue us at extraordinary times, when everything else is beyond man's imagination and beyond his ability to handle the situation, at such times when hopes are low and when we can only perceive a distance so short that we think that at any moment it will all be over. It is at these times that He can stretch the seemingly vanishing time into the distance. The case of my wife stands out as a contemporary example. Most women don't survive the onslaught of high-risk pregnancy or preeclampsia or blood clots to the lungs, but my wife lives not only to tell the story but also so she can renew her love for the Lord and strengthen her faith in Him. Today, just as we tell the story of Job and others mentioned to strengthen our faith, we can also do so by remembering the story of my wife.

When my wife and I began to experience humiliation from our friends and relatives, we were not prepared for such treatment. It was a shameful act and so we reacted harshly. I am sure that if we were accustomed to lawsuits, we would have dragged people to court for their intrusion during every one of those days. We realize now that the Lord was introducing something into our lives that would become a testimony in the form of this book you are now holding in your hands, a book that testifies to His greatness and the working of His miracle. Now we are glad that He has done this for us just as He did for the other children of God mentioned above. We are now able to explain better what the scriptures in the book of James, Acts and others on the subject of "counting it a joy" teach. Many thanks to the Lord for this experience and his guiding hands on my wife.

APPENDIX A
SCRIPTURES

SOME SCRIPTURAL REFERENCES ON GOD'S miracle. All scriptures taken from New King James version.

In John 6:2, the scripture says, *"Then a great multitude followed Him, because they saw His signs which He performed on those who were diseased. He is the same yesterday, today and forever."*

Healing of the blind:

Matthew 9: 27-31: *"When Jesus departed from there, two blind men followed Him, crying out and saying, 'Son of David, have mercy on us.' And when they had come to Him into the house, the blind came to Him. And Jesus said to them, 'Do you believe that I am able to do this?' They said to Him, 'Yes, Lord.' Then He touched their eyes saying, 'According to your faith let it be to you.' And their eyes were opened. And Jesus sternly warned them, saying, 'See that no one knows it.' But when they had departed, they spread the news about Him in all that country."*

Matthew 12:22: *"Then one was brought to Him who was demon-possessed, blind and mute; and He healed him, so that the blind and the mute both spoke and saw."*

Matthew 20: 30; 34: *"And behold two blind men sitting by the road, when they heard that Jesus was passing by, cried out saying, 'Have mercy on us, oh Lord, son of David.' So, Jesus had compassion and touched their eyes. And immediately, their eyes received sight and they followed Him."*

Mark 8: 22-26: *"Then He came to Bethsaida; and they brought a blind man to Him, and begged Him to touch him. So He took the blind man by the hand and led him out of the town. And when He had spit on his eyes and put His hand on him, He asked him if he saw anything. And He looked up and said, 'I see men like trees walking.' Then He put His hands on his eyes again and made him look up. And he was restored and saw everyone clearly. Then He sent him away to his house saying, 'Neither go into the town, nor tell anyone in the town.'"*

Mark 10:51-52: *"So Jesus answered and said to Him, 'What do you want me to do?' The blind man said to Him, 'Rabboni, that I may receive my sight.' Then Jesus said to him, 'Go your way, your faith has made you well.' And immediately he received his sight and followed Jesus on the road."*

Luke 11: 14 *"And He was casting out a demon, and it was mute. So, it was, when the demon had gone out, that the mute spoke; and the multitudes marveled."*

John 9: 6-7: *"When He had said these things, He spat on the ground and made clay with the saliva; and He anointed the eyes of the blind man with the clay. And He said to him, 'Go wash in the pool of Siloam'* (which is translated, sent). *So he went and washed, and came back seeing."*

Victory over death:

Luke 8: 52-55: *"Now all wept and mourned for her; but He said, 'Do not weep; she is not dead, but sleeping.' And they ridiculed Him, knowing that she was dead. But He put them all outside, took her by the hand and called, saying, 'Little girl, arise.' Then her spirit returned, and she arose immediately. And He commanded that she be given something to eat."*

Luke 7: 12-15: *"And when He came near the gate of the city, behold, a dead man was being carried out, the only son of his mother; and she was a widow. And a large crowd from the city was with her. When the Lord saw her, He had compassion on her and said to her, 'Do not weep.' Then He came and touched the open coffin, and those who carried him stood still. And He said, 'Young man, I say to you, arise.' So he who was dead sat up and began to speak. And He presented him to his mother."*

John 11: 38-43: *"Then Jesus, again groaning in Himself, came to the tomb. It was a cave, and a stone lay against it. Jesus said, 'Take away the stone.' Martha, the sister of him who was dead, said to him, 'Lord, by this time there is a stench, for he has been dead four days.' Jesus said to her, 'Did I not say to you that if you would believe you would see the glory of God?' And now when He had said these things, He cried with a loud voice, 'Lazarus, come forth.' And he who had died came out bound hand and foot with grave clothes, and his face was wrapped with a cloth. Jesus said to them, loose him and let him go."*

Matthew 27: 50-62: *"And Jesus cried out again with a loud voice, and yielded up His spirit. Then, behold, the veil of the temple was torn in two from top to bottom; and the earth quaked, and the rocks were split, and the graves were opened; and many bodies of the saints who had fallen asleep were raised;*

and coming out of the graves after His resurrection, they went into the holy city and appeared to many."

Acts 9: 39-40: *"Then Peter arose and went with them. When he had come, they brought him to the upper room. And all the widows stood by him weeping, showing the tunics and garments which Dorcas had made while she was with them. But Peter put them all out, and knelt down and prayed. And turning to the body he said, 'Tabitha, arise.' And she opened her eyes and when she saw Peter she sat up."*

2 Kings 13: 20-21: *"Then Elisha died, and they buried him. And the raiding bands from Moab invaded the land in the spring of the year. So, it was, as they spied a band of raiders; and they put the man in the tomb of Elisha and when the man was let down and touched the bones of Elisha, He revived and stood on his feet."*

Casting out demons:

Matthew 9:32-33: *"And they went out, behold, they brought to Him a man mute, and demon-possessed. And when the demon was cast out, the mute spoke. And the multitudes marveled, saying, 'It was never seen like this in Israel.'"*

Mark 1:23-25: *"Now there was a man in their synagogue with an unclean spirit. And he cried out, saying, 'Let us alone! What have we to do with you, Jesus of Nazareth? Did you come to destroy us? I know who You are the Holy One of God.' But Jesus rebuked him, saying, 'Be quiet, and come out of him!'"*

3. Matthew 8:28;31-32: *"When He had come to the other side, to the country of the Gergesenes, there met Him two demon-possessed men, coming out of the tombs, exceedingly fierce, so that no one could pass that way. So the demons begged Him, saying, 'If You cast us out, permit us to go away into the herd of swine.' And He said to them, 'Go.' So when they had come out, they went into the herd of swine. And suddenly the whole herd of swine ran violently down the steep place into the sea, and perished into the water."*

4. Luke 9:38-42:   *"Suddenly, a man from the multitude cried out, saying, 'Teacher, I implore You, look on my son, for he is my only child. And behold, a spirit seizes him, and he foams at the mouth; and it departs from him with great difficulty, bruising him. So I implored Your disciples to cast it out, but they could not.' Then Jesus answered and said, 'O faithless and perverse generation, how long shall I be with you and bear with you? Bring your son her.' And as he was still coming, the demon threw him down and convulsed him. Then Jesus rebuked the unclean spirit, healed the child, and gave him back to his father."*

How the Lord tamed nature:

Matthew 17:26-27: *"Peter said to Him, 'From strangers.' Jesus said to him, 'Then the sons are free. Nevertheless, lest we offend them. Go to the sea, cast in a hook, and take the fish that comes up first. And when you have opened, you will find a piece of money; take that and give it to them for me and you.'"*

Matthew 21:19: *"And seeing a fig tree by the road, He came to it and found nothing on it but leaves, and said to it, 'Let no fruit grow on you ever again.' Immediately the fig tree withered away."*

John 18:5-6: *"They answered Him. 'Jesus of Nazareth.' Jesus said to them, 'I am He.' And Judas, who betrayed Him, also stood with them. Now when He said to them, 'I am He,' they drew back and fell to the ground."*

4. Luke 9:16-17: *"And He took the five loaves and fish, and looking up to heaven, He blessed and broke them, and gave them to the disciples to set before the multitude. So they all ate and were filled, and twelve baskets of the leftover fragments were taken up by them."*

5. Matthew 8:23-26: *"Now when He got into a boat, His disciples followed Him. And suddenly a great tempest arose on the sea, so that the boat was covered with the waves. But He was asleep. Then His disciples came to Him and awoke Him, saying, 'Lord, save us we are perishing!' But He said to them, 'Why are you fearful, o you of little faith?' Then He arose and rebuked the winds and the sea, and there was a great calm."*

6. Mark 6:49-50: *"And when they saw Him walking on the sea, they supposed it was a ghost, and cried out; for they all saw Him and were troubled. But immediately He talked with them and said to them, 'Be of good cheer! It is I; do not be afraid.'"*

Other healing miracles:

Infirmity:
Luke 13:11-13: *"And behold, there was a woman who had a spirit of infirmity eighteen years, and was bent over and could in no way raise herself up. But when Jesus saw her, He called to him and said to her, 'Woman, you are loosed from your infirmity.' And He laid His hands on her, and immediately she was made straight, and glorified God."*

Cleansing of the ten lepers:
Luke 17:12-14: *"Then as He entered a certain village, there met Him ten men who were lepers, who stood afar off. And they lifted up their voices and said, 'Jesus, Master, have mercy on us.' So when He saw them, He said to them, 'Go show yourselves to the priests.' And so it was that as they went, they were cleansed."*

The powerless:
John 5:6-8: *"When Jesus saw him lying there, and knew that he already*

had been in that condition a long time, He said to him, 'Do you want to be made well?' The sick man answered Him, 'Sir, I have no man to put me into the pool when the water is stirred up; but while I am coming, another steps down before me.' Jesus said to him, 'Rise, take up your bed and walk.'"

Blood problem in women:
Matthew 9:20-22: *"And suddenly, a woman who had a flow of blood for twelve years came from behind and touched the hem of His garment. For she said to herself, 'If only I may touch His garment, I shall be made well.' But Jesus turned around, and when He saw her, He said, 'Be of good cheer Daughter; your faith has made you well.' And the woman was made well from that hour."*

SCRIPTURES QUOTED IN EACH PART:

CHAPTER 1: The Surge of Disorders
- o Isaiah   54: 10
- o Isaiah   43: 2-3
- o Luke   1: 13-17

CHAPTER 3: 23 Days of Resuscitation
- o 1 Thessalonians 5:18
- o Lamentations 3: 13-14
- o Psalm 145:18-19
- o Jeremiah 33:3
- o John 10:27-9
- o Matthew 6:16-18
- o Psalm 55:22
- o Jeremiah 29:11
- o John 20:29
- o John 11:25-26
- o Hebrews 11:1
- o Hebrews 6: 17-18
- o Lamentations 3:57-58
- o Psalms 73:26
- o Isaiah 40:29
- o John 15:7
- o Psalms 103:2-3
- o John 10:27-29
- o Micah 7:7
- o Matthew 26:41

o   I Corinthians 10:13
o   2 Corinthians 1:3-4
o   I Peter 5:8
o   Hebrews 2:18
o   Isaiah 57:18-19
o   Psalm 10:17
o   Jeremiah 29:11
o   Psalm 91:14-15
o   Lamentations 3:21-23
o   James 5:15-16
o   Psalm 147:11
o   Psalm 42:5
o   Isaiah 40:31
o   Psalm 27:14
o   James 1:4-5
o   I Thessalonians 5:11
o   Isaiah 43:2-3
o   Acts 2:28
o   Romans 8:11
o   Matthews 7:7-8
o   Romans 15:4
o   Psalms 125:1
o   Psalms 46:10
o   Job 6:24
o   Job 3:11-12
o   Acts 2:26-28
o   Matthews 7:9-11
o   Job 8:21
o   Jeremiah 30:17
o   Psalms 30:2
o   John 4:7-27
o   Ecclesiastics 12:13
o   Deuteronomy 9:9-18
o   Matthew 4:2
o   1 Kings 19:8
o   Jeremiah 17:10
o   Psalm 18:20

CHAPTER 4: Phase Two of Recovery
o   Romans 5:10
o   1 Thessalonians 5:11
o   Romans 12:1-2

o   Isaiah 50:9
o   Isaiah 55:8-9
o   2 Timothy 1:12
o   2 Corinthians 9:8
o   Matthews 11:28-30
o   Isaiah 42:16
o   Hebrews 6:17-18
o   Romans 12:11
o   Psalms 72:12
o   Deuteronomy 10:21
o   Ephesians 4:31-32

CHAPTER 5:   Northside Rehabilitation Center
o   James 1:12
o   Matthew 25:34-37
o   I John 4:12

CHAPTER 6: Final Discharge
o   1 Peter 1:13
o   Psalm 121:5-8

CHAPTER 7: Another Shock: The Passing of Mom (My Wife's Mother)
o   Ecclesiastics 3:1-2 ; 4
o   John 14:1-2
o   Genesis 9:13-15
o   Matthew 7:7-8
o   Psalm 11:3
o   Matthew 7:21-23
o   1 John 1:1-3
o   Romans 1:16-17
o   Philippians 2:1-8
o   1 Corinthians 12:12-27
o   Acts 4:32-37
o   Hebrews 10:18
o   Acts 2:44-46
o   Galatians 6:9-10
o   Psalm 107:28-30
o   1 Thessalonians 5:17

CHAPTER 8: Benevolence; The Churches' Response to Our Crisis
o   1 Samuel 1:6-7
o   Luke 1:25

o John 3:16
o Ephesians 5:28-33
o Ephesians 5:25
o 1 Corinthians 7:3-5
o 1 Peter 3:7
o Proverbs 5:20
o Matthew 19:5
o Hebrews 13:4
o Mark 10:13-16
o Matthew 18:6
o Mark 9:37
o Genesis 16:21
o Genesis 25:21
o Genesis 30:1
o Judges 13
o 1 Samuel 1
o Luke 1
o Psalm 113:9
o John 16:24
o Mark 11:24
o James 1:12-13
o Psalm 23
o James 1:2
o Acts 5:41

APPENDIX B
PHOTOS

July, 2008
Daniella giving testimony and thanking church members for their prayers during a Sunday morning worship service in Burkina Faso, Ouagadougou, West Africa

Daddy and baby John

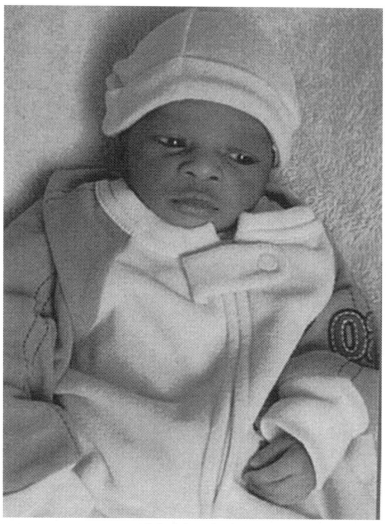

Baby John at birth

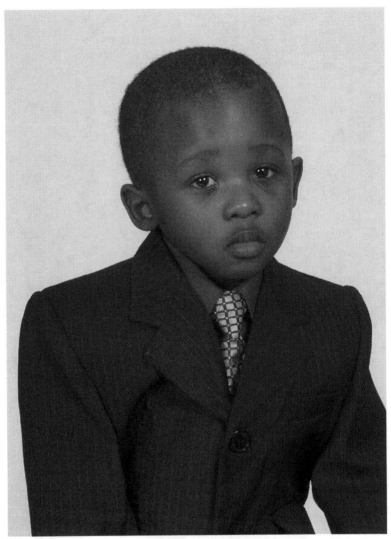

Baby John at age two

Zon and Daniella wedding photo

Daniella's parents

APPENDIX C
HOSPITAL RECORDS

POST-OP CESAREAN SECTION ORDERS
POST-OP DAY ONE ORDERS
Obstetrics

JCMC Cl#: 00915045 MR#: 000405196
PT#: 32904171
QUEWEA ,DANIELLA
DOB: 12/06/07 13:05

PO1000

DATE	PHYSICIAN'S ORDERS

POST-OP CESAREAN ORDERS

1. Bedrest for 8 hours, then stand at bedside
2. Diet: ☐ Clear liquids ☑ Advance as tolerated
3. Maintain Foley, I & O every shift
4. IV: Premixed 0.9% NaCl 1000 mL with Oxytocin 20 units at 125 mL/hour, then D₅LR at 125 mL/hour
5. Pain Medication: ☑ Per anesthesia
   ☐ Demerol 75-100 mg IM every 3 hours PRN pain, when okay with Anesthesia
   ☐ Percocet 5 1 or 2 tablets PO every 4 hours PRN pain, when okay with Anesthesia
   ☐ Naproxen DS 1 PO every 8 hours PRN pain
   ☐ Ibuprofen 600 mg PO every 8 hours PO PRN pain
6. ☐ Promethazine 25 mg every 3 hours PRN nausea: ☐ IV   ☐ IM
   ☑ Zofran 4 mg every 8 hours PRN nausea: ☐ IV   ☐ PO
7. ☑ Ambien ½___ mg PO every night PRN sleep
8. Routine Breast Care   ☐ Lanolin   ☐ Lansinoh
9. CBC post partum Day 1.
10. Give Rh Immune Globulin if mother Rh-negative and baby Rh-positive: ☐
11. If non immune to rubella, give MMR prior to discharge
12. _____
13. _____
14. _____

Physician Signature /M Axell   Date 1 2/7/   Time 0243

POST-OP DAY ONE ORDERS

1. Discontinue IV if tolerating PO liquids and okay with Anesthesia
2. ☐ Simethicone chewable 80 mg PRN gas
   ☐ Bisacodyl suppository if needed for abdominal distention
3. Discontinue Foley catheter
4. ☐ Percocet 5 mg   OR   ☐ Tylenol No. 3   1 or 2 tablets PO every 4 hours PRN pain
   OR   ☐ Lortab 5 1 tablet PO every 4 hours PRN pain (maximum 8 tablets/day)
5. ☐ Naproxen DS 1 PO every 8 hours PRN pain
   OR   ☐ Ibuprofen 600 mg PO every 8 hours PRN pain
6. _____
7. _____

Physician Signature _____ Date _____ Time _____

Place an 'X' in the
box for STAT

FORM NO. SO-0491   Rev. 02/13/06   Scan Orders to Pharmacy before placing in Medical Record.

Post-op cesarean orders record

Zon G. Quewea

QUEWEA, DANIELLA A, Enc #32904171 OBT 12/6/2007 Procedure Data

Quewea, Daniella
MR# 405196
Pt# 32904171

12/06/07 15:00 EST

Johnson City, TN 37604

INTRAOPERATIVE RECORD   Page 2 (EOD)

All care provided per MSHA policy and AORN recommended practices.
Blanks are not applicable to this patient's care.

Instrument Count 1: Correct	Sponge Count 1: Correct	Needles/Blades Count 1: Correct	Towel Count 1: Correct
Instrument Count 2: Not Done	Sponge Count 2: Not Done	Needles/Blades Count 2: Not Done	Towel Count 2: Not Done
Instrument Count 3: Correct	Sponge Count 3: Correct	Needles/Blades Count 3: Correct	Towel Count 3: Correct
Instrument Count 4: Not Done	Sponge Count 4: Not Done	Needles/Blades Count 4: Not Done	Towel Count 4: Not Done

Performed by: Count #1: Billie K Peters LPN   Michelle A Hogan RN   Count #2:

Count #3:   Count #4:

Surgeon Notified of Counts: Yes

Meds other than by Anesthesia: Heparin _____ units/ml ___ given   Thrombin _____   Xylocaine: ___ % Xylocaine ___ ml given
_____ ml injected by _____

Irrigations: 0.9% NaCl (#L used): 1   H2O (#L used):
Antibiotic: ancef 2 grams

Family contact made at: incision
Implants: Device: Manufacturer: Lot#/Ser#   Model#/Cat#   Quantity: Location:

Equipment: Patient temperature monitored by Anesthesia
Laser Type: Padded K-thermia on bed @   degrees F
ESU #1:04AGS006   Pad site 1: rt thigh   Applied by: _____   Preop skin condition: clear
Skin Prep Prior to Tape Placement: Allkare
Type of Tape: Medipore
Dressings: Telfa,ABD

Post-operative Patient Assessment and Discharge Condition

Postop Ground Pad #1 Site Condition:clear
Postop Skin Prep Site(s) Condition: clear   Postop Positioning Aid Site Condition:clear
Postop Wound Classification: I - Clean
Postop Status: Warm,Dry,Pink,Asleep   Other:
From OR Table: Four-Man
Evaluation/Outcome   A. No evidence of redness, skin breakdown or other injury related to surgical or anesthesia event.
                      B. Principles of asepsis and skin prep performed per policy. No evidence of surgery related infection.
Discharged To: Patient Room   Other: 1507   Method of Transport: Bed
Transported with: Report given/called to:
Nurses Notes:

Intra-operative record

182

BIBLIOGRAPHY

WEBSITE SOURCES:

Burke, Cormac. Marriage and Family in Africa, April 1988, *http://www.cormacburke.or.ke/node/637*

Bales, Norman. Does Egalitarian Marriage Work and is it Biblical? Vol.3, num.16, May 13th, 1998. *http://www.allaboutfamilies.org/98aaf16.html*

Leslie Lafayette, Founder of Childfree Network Organization of America *http://findarticles.com/p/articles/mi_m4021/is_n4_v18/ai_18142070/pg_1*

Preeclampsia Foundation: Non-profit Organization, support safe pregnancy, fund

Research on Preeclampsia and support awareness on the disorder *http://www.preeclampsia.org/index.asp*

Oral Anticoagulant Research and Resources for Patients and Caregiver

Food and Drug Administration Information

Focus on Genetic Testing on Coumadin *http://www.mybloodthinner.org/research.htm*

Riedmann, Peter. The Christian Way of Life, Community of Goods *http://www.anabaptistchurch.org/christianlife.htm*

Kishindo, Paul. Family Planning and the Malawian Male. Nordic Journal of African Studies. 4(1): 26-34(1995)

University of Malawi, Malawi
  http://www.njas.helsinki.fi/pdf/vol4num1/kishindo.pdf

The Ghanaian Family Structure, Life and Formation.
  http://family.jrank.org/pages/710/Ghana.html

BOOKS:

Price, Charles S. The Real Faith for Healing. Edited and Rewritten by Harold J.

Chadwick. North Brunswick, NJ. Bridge-Logos Publishers, 1997

Schaefer, Richard T. Sociology Eight Edition. New York, NY McGraw-Hill Companies, Inc., 2003

MacNUTT, Francis. The Prayers That Heals: Praying for Healing in the Family Notre Dame, Indiana. Ave Maria Press, 1983

Altma, Roberta. Waking up Fighting Back: The Politics of Breast Cancer. Little, Brown & Company, 1996

Lamanna, Mary Ann & Riedmann, Agnes. Marriages and Families: Making Choices in A Diverse Society. Wadworth, 2000

Wells, Gibson J. Current Issues in Marriages and Family, Second Edition Macmillan Publishing Company, New York, NY. 1979

Landis, Paul H. Social Problems in Nation and World Chicago, Philadelphia; New York; Lippicott Co., 1959

SUGGESTED READING:
HIGH-RISK PREGNANCY:

David James, Philip Steer, Carl Weiner and Bernard Gonik. High Risk Pregnancy: Text book with CD-ROM, August, 2005

Elizabeth S. Gilbert-RNC, MS, & FNPC: Manual of High Risk Pregnancy and Delivery November, 2006

John T. Queenan, Catherine Y. Spong & Charles J. Lockwood. Management of High Risk Pregnancy, an Evidence-based Approach, June, 2007

John T. Queenan, Cahtherine Y. Spong & John C. Hobbins: Protocols for High-Risk Pregnancy, November 2005

Errol Norwitz and RN, Diana Raab. Your High Risk-Pregnancy: Practical, Supportive Guide, June 2000

Elizabeth Platt, Andrea Tetreau, NP, Michael G. Pinette, 100 Questions and Answers About your High-Risk Pregnancy, June, 2006

Denise M. Chism. High-Risk Pregnancy Sourcebook, May 1998

John T. Queenan. High-Risk Pregnancy, June, 2007

PREECLAMPSIA:

Lyall, Fiona and Belfort, Michael. Pre-eclampsia: Etiology and Clinical Practices June, 2007

Davis, Denise. Baby Nathan, October, 2007

Qontro Medical Guides: Preeclampsia Medical Guide, July 2008

Preeclampsia: Webster's Time Line History, 1951-2007

Icon Group International, July, 2008

Baker, Philip & Kingdom, John C.P. Pre-eclampsia: Current Perspectives on Management, December, 2003

Wilson, Rhoda. Recurrent Miscarriage and Preeclampsia: Roles Played by the Immune System and Antioxidants, October, 2004

21st Century Complete Medical Guide to Preeclampsia, Eclampsia, Toxemia of Pregnancy, Authoritative Government Documents, Clinical...for Patients and Physicians (CD-ROM): PM Medical Health News, June, 2004

Tucker, Miriam E. Obesity doesn't push Mild Hypertension to Preeclampsia Women's Health: An Article From Family Practice News, April, 2005(Digital)

Zoler, Mitchel L.: Obesity-Preeclampsia Linkage May be Vascular. Vessel Information Might Increase Risk by Releasing Reactive Oxygen Species and Immunostimulants (Ob...An Article From Family Practice News, September, 2006(Digital).

Johnson, Kate. High Sugar, Fat Intake in Early Pregnancy Tied to Preeclampsia. (Brief Article) (Statistical Data Included). An Article From: Family Practice News(Digital), June 2005

HIGH BLOOD PRESSURE:

Townsend, Raymond. 100 Q & A About High Blood Pressure (Hypertension) Sudbury, Mass. Jones & Bartlett Publisher, 2008

Hart, Tudor Julian, Fahey Tom, Savage Wendy. High Blood Pressure at Your Fingertips: The Comprehensive And Medically Accurate Manual on How to Manage Your High Blood Pressure. Netlibrary, Inc. London; Class 1999

High Blood Pressure(Hypertension): USA Food and Drug Administration Office of Women's Health; National Government Publication. Rockville, MD. FDA Office of Women's Health, 2007

Bauer, Brent A.; Mayo Clinic; Galam Media. Mayo Clinic Wellness Solutions for High Blood Pressure. Rochester, MN: Mayo Clinic, (US) Galam, 2007

Fahey Tom; Murphy Deirdre; Hart Tudor Julian; Netlibrary, Inc. High Blood Pressure. eBook Document. London Class, 2004

Primary Prevention of Hypertension: Clinic and Public Health Advisory From the National High Blood Pressure Education Program. National Government Publication. Microfiche. By National High Blood Pressure Education Program National Heart Lung & Blood Institute. Bethesda, MD. USA Dept. of Health & Human Services, National Institute of Health, National Lung and Blood Institute, 2002

Rubin, Alan L. High Pressure for Dummies: New York, NY Wiley Pub., 2002

Koop Everett, C. & Matson Boyd. High Blood Pressure:

VHS, VIDEO:

New York NY Time Life Medical 1996

Sheps, Sheldon G. Mayo Clinic on High Blood Pressure

Rochester, Minn. Mayo Clinic, 2002

CLINICAL DEATH:

Bremmer, Patricia A. Clinical Death

Venango, NE: Windcall Enterprises, 2008

Rando, Therese A. Grief, Dying, And Death: Clinical Intervention For Caregivers Champaign, Ill. Research Press Co., 1984

Brubaker, Don. Absent From The Body: One Man's Clinical Death, A Journey Through Heaven And Hell. Palmetto, Fla. Peninsula Pub., 1996

Peter Safar; et al. Reversibility of Clinical Death: Symposium on Resuscitation Research, International Resuscitation Research Center, University of Pittsburg, PA. Baltimore, MD Williams and Wilkins, 1988

Samuel S. Chugh; et al. Epidemiology of Sudden Cardiac Death Clinical And Research Implication Philadelphia, PA (etc.) W.B Saunders Co. etc

BLOOD CLOTS:

Hampton, Tracy. Sarcomas And Blood Clots Chicago: American Medical Association, 1966-

Ann K. Wittkowsky. United States Agency For Healthcare Research And Quality. Your Guide to Preventing And Treating Blood Clots.

Rockville, MD. US Dept. of Health & Human Services, Agency For Healthcare Research And Quality, 2008

Maureen Andrew; NetLibrary, Inc. Blood Clots And Strokes A Guide For Parents And Little Folks, Hamilton, Ont. BC Decker, 1998

Seppa, Nathan: Sticky Platelets Boost Blood Clots Washington D.C Science Service, 1966-